DOWN ON THE FARM

Real Life Stories and Photographs by a Minnesota Farm Girl

JESSICA CALLENS

Morgan James Publishing • NEW YORK

Real Life Stories and Photographs by a Minnesota Farm Girl

Jessica Callens

Copyright ©2006 Jessica Callens

ISBN: 1-60037-150-7 (Hardcover)
ISBN: 1-60037-002-0 (Paperback)

Published by:

MORGAN · JAMES
THE ENTREPRENEURIAL PUBLISHER™
www.morganjamespublishing.com

Morgan James Publishing, LLC
1225 Franklin Ave Ste 32
Garden City, NY 11530-1693
Toll Free 800-485-4943
www.MorganJamesPublishing.com

Cover/Interior Design by:
Rachel Campbell
rcampbell77@cox.net

Habitat
for Humanity®
Peninsula
Building Partner

 **TO** my parents Frederick and Sandra
And the entire Callens Gang
For your love, encouragement, patience,
and most of all for giving me the wonderful
opportunity of living in the country

TO Aunt Anet
For nurturing my love of writing

TO Cousin George
Who helped make my dreams come true

TABLE of CONTENTS

SPRING FEVER AND THE MUD PUD BLUES···1

THE GREAT QUEST···7

AUCTION ADVENTURE···13

A STORY OF SOWDATION···19

DADDY'S LITTLE HELPER···23

WISDOM WRUNG FROM THE WRINGER···27

WHEN CITY MEETS COUNTRY···33

BARN DANCE···37

READY-SET-STUCCO···41

RODEO TIME···45

DISASTER IN THE PARLOR···49

FARM LIFE: THE REAL LIFE···55

THE PLENTIFUL VEGETABLE WOES···59

CANNING-WELL WORTH THE EFFORT···65

AN OLD FARMER···69

THE MIDNIGHT MASSACRE···73

NEW GAL'S ON THE FARM···79

CHRISTMAS IN THE COUNTRY···85

A CHRISTMAS GOOSE···89

'TIS THE SEASON···93

HE WAS LAID IN OUR MANGER···99

ABOUT THE AUTHOR···105

CHAPTER 1

Spring Fever and the Mud Pud Blues

An old and familiar plague is sweeping the country, friends. And though many times we have caught it, we will never be quite immune to its grasping fingers. It is Spring Fever of which I speak, folks, and what are the symptoms? Hmmm there are quite a few.....convulsive browsing of seed catalogues, fitful scrubbing of floors and windows, vigorous emptying of cupboards, closets and drawers and many more strange proceedings. Have you caught it? Well don't be alarmed, as you certainly aren't the only one.

On the farm, Spring Fever usually comes by way of the wind. It is impossible not to catch it on the delicious breezes scented with warming earth, and melting water. The warmth of the sun enlarges the symptoms rather alarmingly, as does the disappearance of dirty snow. Spring Fever is not at all dangerous and can be decidedly pleasant - when diagnosed correctly. I have been told that it never goes away until the coming of summer, but can be greatly minimized by certain activities. When you have finished your extensive scourge of the messy indoors, starting on the outdoors keeps your pent up energies from doing damage elsewhere. Oh yes, there is plenty for an energetic person to do out of doors. The raking up of last Falls leaves that have been stuck under the snow banks, trimming away at the trees whose branches may have bowed under the weight of winter snow, disposing of sickly indoor plants and a score of other little outlets for Spring Fever vigor.

Now I must confess that a most unfortunate companion of Spring Fever is none other than the dreaded Mud Pud blues. There is no easier way to catch it than to discover your immaculate white kitchen floor spread with a disastrous series of black marks in an assortment of boot shapes. (By the way - white tile in a farm kitchen was a *big* mistake!) Oh those Mud Pud blues!

Anxious to discover the culprit who brought the blues into our house, I didn't have to search long before I found 7 children guilty of the charge. And I didn't even have to ask for their individual interpretations, they did not hold back any information (excuses!). It seems one set of boot prints where from a child in need of warm milk. "Aw Jess, I needed to use the stove to heat up the lambs bottle!" "Why didn't you re-move your boots before entering the clean kitchen?" "I was in a hurry; the lamb was hungry!" My irritation was fading fast.....but *then*- the boys admitted to trespassing simply because of a sudden craving for crackers. My dander was up again! "Mom made a huge dinner, you guys! How could you *possibly* be hungry after all that food?!" (If I recall correctly, it was a dinner of ham steaks, green beans, baked potatoes, beets and coconut pie!) "That wasn't enough to hold me until supper Jess, and neither are these crackers. Is there any pie left?" I couldn't help smiling. Would the boys' appe-tites *ever* be satisfied?

I soon discovered that the littlest tracks, conspicuous because they were made with bare feet, belonged to the baby. (The youngest is always considered the baby until a new addition arrives.) She seemed to have stepped out of doors when mommy wasn't looking and had a nice little "tramp". I gave her a kiss. Even babies aren't immune to Spring Fever I guess! Eventually all the stories came out, and the humor of the situ-ation got the better of my Mud Pud blues. I put on a stern face though (as stern as I could manage, viewing their mud smudged faces) and told them that under no circumstance were they to put a foot - *or* a boot, on the kitchen floor. And for good measure, (you never can tell when the boys will be hungry again) I locked the front door.

The mud and puddles were unavoidable the day we moved sows. As the result of a unanimous vote, we stood ankle deep in mud hurrying to move sows as a surprise for dad. We wanted to have the job all done for him when he got home from work. The afternoon sunlight slanted down, and it was a beautiful day.....unless you had the Mud Pud blues. I guess we were too busy dealing with ornery sows to mind the mud at first, but we began to consider it as a serious opposition to our plans when mom hooked the skid loader up to the livestock trailer. The van would never make it through all that mud between the buildings, so the loader was our only alternative. Mom backed slowly in-between the granary and sow barn, only yelling in fright once or twice as the wheels spun in the black muck. We all held our breath as the wheel ruts got deeper and the mud flew higher but soon she had the trailer backed up to the big gate.

It only took a few minutes for us to decide that it was totally out of the question to move 11 sows each weighing around 450 lbs into a rusty 16' livestock trailer under the muddy conditions. Another important point to consider was that the livestock trailer belonged to my uncles.....I had visions of us returning it with the bottom dropped out from the weight of the sows. So we loaded only 6 surprisingly *willing* (thank goodness!) sows into the waiting "rattletrap" (sorry uncles!) and decided we would make another trip for the remaining 5. Do you suppose the sows knew that our new Poland China boar was waiting in the new quarters?

The situation as always was not without its humor. Only this time it wasn't on my side. As my sister threw back her head and giggled uncontrollably at me, I could only guess how spattered my face must have been by that time. We all were covered with mud, and a suspicious odor suggested that mud was not the only ornament plastering our coveralls. Ah well, no time to indulge in the Mud Pud blues.

Mom and the trailer slid and skid down to the new sow pen where we discovered that dad himself had unknowingly hindered our efforts. That morning he had cleaned out the pen (Spring Fever?) with the skid loader making a manure pile near the very entrance that the sows needed to be loaded through. He had been in a hurry and intended on hauling it much farther away when he got home. Well a manure pile wasn't about to stop mom after she'd gotten this far, so she angled the trailer a bit and rolled right over part of the manure pile. She ended up with just enough space to straighten out behind it. The sows were successfully unloaded (I suspect they rather enjoyed the bumpy ride) and we repeated the loading and hauling process all over again with the remaining 5.

When dad arrived at home that evening, the only traces of our secret surprise were the huge ruts in the mud going from the old sow pen to the new, and half a flattened manure pile. Nonetheless he was pleasantly surprised, and seeing him happy (and the nice hot shower I had) erased all traces of the Mud Pud blues.

As a result of Spring Fever the "pleasant epidemic", we had a little cook-out the other night. What memories of summers gone by and anticipation for this coming one filled my mind. I can't help but wish summer was here......even though March, which is often said to be our biggest snow month, is just arriving. But dreaming nice *warm* thoughts of summer helps chase away the Mud Pud blues that are inevitable when - you trip and fall in the mud carrying a 5 gallon pail of water to the hogs, you discover half way through a puddle that there was a hidden hole in the bottom of your rubbers, the horse kicks up her hooves and sends mud flying in your face when you gallop her, you have to help your little sister out of a sticky spot and end up leaving your boots stuck in the muck along with hers, the dog puts perfect paw prints on your Sunday coat, and yes, even when your clean kitchen floor is clean no longer!

CHAPTER 2
The Great Quest

It's a food; it's thin, green and purple. It grows among the grass in ditches, OR in the gardens of those who are crazy about it. What *is* this illusive thing that seekers will put aside all thought of wood ticks while they swim through the grass to find it and drivers nearly steer into the ditch while scanning the grassy area for it? With May comes the great quest for.... the *asparagus plant*!

Now you're thinking one of two things: EWWWWW!!! *Asparagus!* Or, MMMMMMM! *Asparagus!!!!* Well whether you're an asparagus lover or *not* you've got to admit that nothing quite compares with the sport of Asparagus hunting! And if you've never tried it, you'll soon find out why so many take this spring sport so seriously. You dedicated hunters know what I'm talking about. Oh the glory of getting to that huge plant *first*—even before your eagle-eyed neighbor! The secret delight in knowing of a hidden plant along some deserted country road, the delicious, reckless feeling that comes with using up a whole tank of gas cruising the back roads searching for asparagus, and then of course, the thumbing through cookbooks to find just the *perfect* asparagus recipe (or if you're like us-2 or 3 good recipes).....oh *yeah*!

And the fun is just beginning! While we've had asparagus (nearly 100 plants to be exact) already growing for some time in our gardens this spring, the ditch asparagus is just popping up. My sister and I rode Star down the road a couple evenings ago to check out one "spot"and found just a few spears. With a little more rain and sunshine, asparagus hunting will soon begin in earnest! You folks who are totally new to this *crazy* (that's what you're thinking, right?) scheme called "asparagus hunting," must really be puzzled by now! Let me share with you what a day of hunting for this special plant might be like if you were along with our gang. Nothing can compare with the excitement of a real asparagus quest!

It's a warm day in later May; school is out so we begin our quest early in the morning before the sun becomes too hot. We all jump into the van and mom gets into the drivers seat (I don't want the boring job of *driving*!) and we're ready to go! Wait..... no, we're *not* ready. Roll call everyone! Everyone calls off their birth status: "1, 2,, 3 ...5,6,7,8........" Hold on a minute! Where's Marisa? Apparently not quite through with breakfast. Alright.....5 precious minutes lost. We're ready to roll again, only- "MOM!" (Brakes slam on and everyone is jolted forward. "I forgot my shoes!" Mom looks around until her eyes rest on one of the older kids. "Yeah, I was supposed to get his shoes....." the guilty one admits. We back rather crookedly up the driveway to the house and someone gets Caleb's shoes out of the entryway. NO MORE INTERUPTIONS. IF YOU'RE BAREFOOT - YOU'LL HAVE TO DEAL WITH IT! No one complains, we're raring to get out into those ditches! Now we're *really* on our way! Slowly we drive along until: "I SEE one!" (*Slam*, go the brakes, *bang*, go the car doors) and 7 kids swarm the ditch vying for the honored position of "mom's best asparagus hunter".

Since none of us want to search for ticks in Bella's diaper when the hunt is over, she stays in the car with mom. The scrambling begins while admonitions to "be careful" are heard from the car. We come up without a scratch - except those from the grass and dead twigs, and one on my arm from Silvana's nails. Without a bug - except for a few ticks, a couple lady bugs and the daddy long legs crawling up Claytons back, and WITH a bunch of asparagus!!   Mom begins filling the basket next to her on the passenger seat and soon we're on our way again.

This seems to be a "hot spot" so instead of climbing in the car and tripping over each other to jump out every two minutes, we simply walk the whole ditch. We split up, 4 kids in the ditch across the road and 3 in the other. Occasional victorious cries are heard from the other "team" now and then, and once in a while a disappointing *"someone's been here first!"*. The sun gets higher and the basket is overflowing with green spears. Marisa locates a tick on her leg and I begin to feel rather itchy from imaginary ones. Occasionally our eyes are drawn from the grassy ditches to look at the beautiful blue sky, and a few times I even stray from the *real* quest to gather some lovely wildflowers.

Hmm....this next road seems to be a dud. Everyone loads into the van. Each one of us is tired, but no one wants to be the first to admit it. After all.....a mighty asparagus hunter (especially mom's *best* asparagus hunter) mustn't show signs of fatigue. Oh *no*. That would be just totally *sissy*. We travel along at the rather speedy (for asparagus hunting) rate of 25 MPH since some of the little ones have begun to get hungry, and like a bunch of young hawks, we scour the entire ditch territory with our eyes.   Suddenly, everyone's ears prick up and we lean forward straining to see a stopped vehicle in the distance. Grim looks are exchanged as we silently acknowledge the existence of a competitor.   We drive by *trying* not to stare, *trying* not to see his satisfied grin, and *trying* hardest of all not to see if he's gathering a lot. The only comments from the back seats are: "Man, why did he have to get there first?" "Did you see how many he was holding? I bet there were more than a dozen in his hand!" "He sure looked pleased with himself too........" From the front seat: *"Kids!!"* We glance sheepishly at each other and then of one accord, look at the brimming, bulging, overflowing basket in the front, and grin.

Finally everyone gives up and admits that they are "starving to death" and ply mom with requests for lunch. Only this time there are no arguments to settle. A unanimous "let's have asparagus and pasta!" from the back of the van, settles everything. At home we de-tick and de-grass ourselves, then begin to count the bountiful basket of "loot". Some of it will be eaten fresh, but most of it is frozen or canned for the winter months. As pound after pound is added up on the kitchen table I begin to feel guilty about the guy with his dozen spears. But who knows...... he probably had a basket hidden on his front seat and felt sorry for this bunch of youngsters staring dolefully at him! If he only knew that it was the largest, toughest, asparagus hunting gang in the county that passed him on the road, he might have thought *differently.*

CHAPTER 3
Auction Adventure

Who knows the excitement of attending an auction? What pastime (besides asparagus hunting of course) can compare with browsing through the many items listed on a sale bill? What brightens the human eye more thoroughly than the discovery of interesting thing-a-ma-jigs, what-cha-ma-callits, do-dingers and what-nots listed for sale? Let me tell you my friends, there is something so extraordinary about a sale or auction that it lightens even the heaviest and dullest of hearts, the drowsiest minds and brightens the most placid countenances.

The Sunday morning dawned, not the usual "bright and clear" bur rather, rainy and foggy. I was awfully disappointed that it should rain on the morning of the big auction (I assumed it was big from the enormous sale bill) and even had second thoughts about attending. But I was determined to tag along with dad to experience an auction no matter what the weather, and my sisters were equally determined to tag along with me. So, we bundled ourselves into sweatshirts, raincoats and rubbers, and braved the chilly dampness of the great outdoors. I began to seriously doubt if there would be any sale after all, but dad seemed cheerfully confident that neither rain, nor frigid temperatures, raw wind, snow nor really any sort of nasty weather, could daunt the spirit of faithful auction goers. We soon realized that he was correct as we approached the long lines of cars near the farm auction site.

Our excitement mounted as we sloshed our way up to the buildings and curiously examined several large farm items. Dad peered out from under the hood of his poncho, his keen eyes scanning the hog equipment and making mental notes. The only mental note I was taking, was on the absence of a suitable rest-room. "Dad, do women ever go to these auctions?" I asked. He replied that they sometimes did, but that didn't put my fears to rest. We wandered past a barn stopping to check over some gates, old milk machines, and fence-posts. I caught sight of the owner of the farm whose property was being auctioned off. A slight damper was put on my excitement as I glimpsed the tired, bent form and sad face of the man. How many years had he lived here, loved here, and raised a family here on his beloved farm? What items up for sale were connected with a precious memory, a happy moment gone by? It was not only a lifetime's collection of "things" being auctioned off, it was an actual lifetime. We passed each other and I greeted him with a handshake and a smile of encouragement.

As we continued on, the house came into view along with (to my great relief) a porta-pottie. I relaxed considerably, and we entered a building where most of the auction goers seemed to be congregating. Three hayracks completely covered with thing-a-ma-jigs and all the above mentioned, took up most of the room and a pleasant buzz of voices filled the air. At least it's dry in here, I thought as I put down my hood so I could see things better. My sisters and I followed dad about the crowded building like four young ducklings and a gander, oooing, aahhing and asking silly questions. "What in the world is this gadget dad?" "Dad, is this a guillotine?" Smothering a laugh, "No little girlie, it's a double bladed ax." "Betcha don't know what this is." I challenged my sister pointing to an object on one of the hay racks. She looked perplexed as she examined a rusty sort of greenish grating with a bent arm on it. "It's a step for a John Deere tractor!" I exclaimed triumphantly, having identified at least one object in the amazing jumble.

I looked around at all the people pressing forward as the auctioneer took his place on a hay rack. Some had the appearance of experienced auction veterans. Their shrewd, business like glances took in the best bargains and most practical objects, mentally discarding the rest. Still they were not above the festivity of the occasion, and there was a visible gleam in the eyes of even the crustiest old characters. Then there were those that appeared less frugal, reasoning that it wouldn't hurt to add this little thing or that little thing to a larger collection of "things" at home. What was a buck or two or three (or four, or five or six!) when it came to some unknown rarity? And of course there were those extremely excited looking folks who eagerly pawed through everything- plastic bottle caps, rusted wire, old bike chains, it didn't matter. They were there to bid, bid, bid, just for the sheer joy of doing so. These were "new" auction goers, I concluded, who were very enthusiastic about their first experience. AND of course there were the jolly, rolly polly gentleman hanging out around the concession stand. We all know why *they* were there.

The auctioneer began his rhythmic chant and the bidding began. It was some unusual bidding too! In fact, you could hardly tell that someone had bid at all until they were handed the purchased item. When dad was suddenly handed a box of nice looking screwdrivers without my having noticed a movement from him, I was determined to look harder. Over to my right a man gently nodded his head at the auctioneer's assistant, and another barely raised a thumb above his waist. I began to be afraid to scratch my nose in case the auctioneer mistook it for a bid! Every time I would rub my cheek or something the auctioneer seemed to look at me to ascertain whether or not I was bidding, so I tried to be careful and move my hands only in between the selling of items. Perhaps I was being overcautious, but I didn't want to get stuck paying for a bucket of rusty bolts or something similarly useless to a girl. Gone are the days when I used to string bolts on twine for a necklace, and those were the shiny new ones anyway.

I moved closer to dad and kept one eye trained on him, and one on the auctioneer. Before long I saw him hold up a hand and a few flips of the wrist later we were the possessors of eight, 5 gallon buckets full of miscellaneous...........things. "It's a good thing you brought us along dad!" I teased him as we girls lugged the buckets out to the van. The rain was still pouring down and it seemed to have been hours since we arrived. Still the auctioneer's voice droned on while he sold off the small items. The little concession stand in one corner was causing my stomach to utter mysterious rumblings and I telegraphed my wishes to all three sisters. (Discreetly of course!) Just a dramatic roll of the eyes towards the food and back again to my stomach. I guess dad could tell by the way we looked that lunchtime had been quite a few hours ago and told us to go buy something we wanted. A Snickers bar later and I felt refreshed enough to peel my eyes away from the food and take more interest in the proceedings of the auction itself.

I couldn't help but smile to myself at the excitement of one fellow who purchased a battered sort of machine that appeared to be as un-useful as it was unidentifiable. (Maybe Identifiable by persons aged 90 and up.) Immediately afterwards I felt a bit of remorse as he lovingly patted his new gadget. A satisfied bidder shouldered a small ax, and two bidders vying for an antique sign, stared each other down across the hayrack. The loser tried to hide a disappointed look as the price shot above his range, but I could see his eyes linger on the quaint sign as it's new owner gently handled it. The bidding continued and we made several more trips to the van with dad carrying the heavy objects. After a while it occurred to me that my rain coat was not quite as rain proof as I had thought it. Dampness seeped through two coats and a sweatshirt until I was quite chilled. All of my sisters appeared to be in quite the same condition, but the excitement of an auction isn't something to be given up in a hurry.

There was a change of scene as the auctioneer moved his speaker out into the yard and began auctioning off the shovels, picks, spades and pitch-forks that lined the outside wall of a building. Since many of the men interested in those items surrounded the auctioneer and towered above us blocking our vision, we girls amused ourselves by comparing footprints in the mud. It was interesting to see old friends standing about with their hands in their pockets visiting about corn prices, weather, crops, and many other such topics. Every now and then one or the other would take a pinch of "sneuss" or complacently shoot a brown spurt of tobacco into an equally brown puddle. (I took care to stay very much out of the way!) Eager young bidders stood about grinning and comparing notes.

Well, time went on and when our clothes became too wet for endurance, and our limbs too shaky to endure US, we went home leaving dad as a more seasoned auction goer, to continue watching the interesting proceedings. Everyone at home got a glowing account of the exciting happenings of the auction, because over a bowl of hot chicken soup, who can remember the wet and chilly part of it all?

CHAPTER 4
A Story of "Sowdation"

nce in a while there comes a time when modern medicines just don't do the trick. Sometimes that dusty bottle with the rusted cap way back on the cobwebby shelf contains just exactly what you need to cure an ailment. And not only may that old bottle of cure-all be good for you, it just might be the right thing for your animals as well. We recently found out just how potent an old bottle of "stuff" can really be!

The new mother sow stood there on the mound of straw growling and grunting angrily at her new baby piglets. We all glanced worriedly at one another. This would never do. This mother's attitude plainly said: "Outa my way kids! I don't want to feed you! I don't want to snuggle with you! I just don't want you in my life!" And folks, there is just no changing a mother sows mind. When she doesn't want to lie down and let her piglets drink, they simply aren't going to get a drink. We clearly needed some kind of a sedative if we were going to keep the new arrivals from starving to death. Ideas began to form and we exchanged them. "An injection might do it." "Maybe we could just knock her out!" "How about tying her down?" "Better put a muzzle on her then!" "Maybe we could all sit on her to hold her still!" "Whatever we do we better be gentle. These hogs are marketed in the finest restaurants as natural, un-bruised and un-blemished pork!" All through this repartee Dad stood silent. Suddenly he chuckled. "By golly, I think I've got the answer." Without responding to the bombardment of questions, he headed for the house. We followed expectantly.

Down to the basement we went, straight to the cupboard storing canned vegetables, fruits and dad's homemade Elderberry wine. Dad reached way into the back past the pears, beans and tomatoes, past the gleaming jars of jelly and right past the Elderberry wine. What suspense! We held our breaths as he rummaged around and appeared to grasp something. What was it he brought forth into the light of the single bulb? Nothing but one of those almost forgotten bottles of Crab Apple wine. We gasped! Dad brushed the dust off the bottle and held the sparkling liquid up to the light. "Was a bad batch to begin with," he commented. "Pretty sour and quite a few years old, but I'm not about to use my good Elderberry on a hog!" "You're going to give wine to the sow, dad?" "Yes I am, and I bet it'll work too!" Of course! We all looked at each other. What better a sedative than wine!

Out to the sow pen we trouped, dad in the lead with the bottle of Crab Apple Wine. He dumped the entire contents into the trough of the troublesome sow. She came immediately out of her hut to bark at us, but as the pungent scent of vinegary, fermented crab apples filled the barn, she turned her attention to the trough. That sow plunged her nose into the wine and drank every last drop within a matter of minutes. The whole quart! We looked for signs of sleepiness, drowsiness or slowed breathing, but there weren't any. She even appeared to be able to walk in a straight line if you didn't count that decided wiggle of the hind-quarters she inherited from her mamma. The sow looked up at us and begged for more.

As one, we all looked at dad. He scratched his head. "She's such a big animal I guess it's going to take a little more kids." He went back to the house and returned carrying two more jugs of Crab Apple Wine. There was a funny expression on his face. "You know what? That wine sure has improved with age! I can hardly believe it's the same batch I pushed to the back shelf a few years ago. I sure hate to waste it on this sow!" The sow drank 3 whole quarts of wine before she yawned contentedly and waddled into her hut. Loud snores issued from within and the piglets saw their chance. We all grinned happily as they guzzled down that life-saving milk.

They all slept peacefully that night I'm sure, the mamma with a bellyful of wine and the babies with a bellyful of milk. The funny thing about the whole deal is that while our intention was to sedate that sow once, she is now permanently sedated. You never saw such a calm, gentle mamma happily feeding her piglets day after day. She's a new hog! And all because of a dose of that old Crab Apple wine!

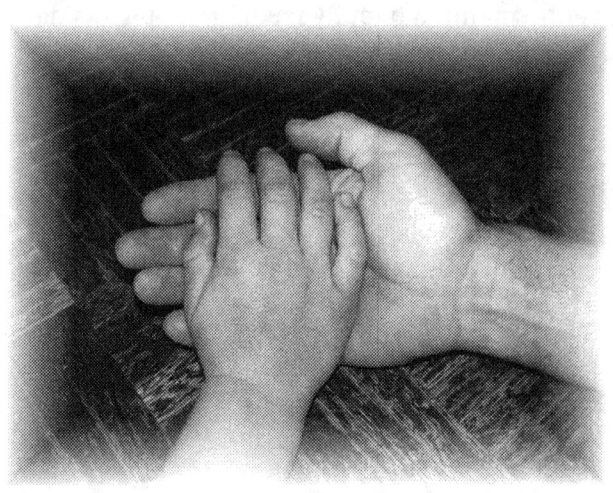

CHAPTER 5
Daddy's Little Helper

For my little brother Caleb who is daddy's little helper

Ruddy cheeks and tousled hair
brow unblemished by work or care.
Eager smile and a willing hand,
he try's so hard to be a man.

2. Daddy's pounding nails today,
he goes to help instead of play.
The biggest grin is on his face,
when daddy ties his pouch in place.

3. He pounds so hard to be just like dad,
but there's a bit more muscle to be had.
Daddy comes to give a hand
'cause he's the strongest in the land!

4. *That is how it appears to he,*
who "just like daddy", wants to be.
Dad says eat all the beans you can
then you'll grow up to be a man!

5. *When daddy drives that big old Case,*
the seat of honor is his place.
Daddy's lap is where he rides,
and goes along to help him drive.

6. *A carefree look is on his face,*
you know he'd have no other place.
"Daddy needs my help" says he,
and daddy doesn't disagree.

7. *Now it's time to move some hogs,*
it's right by daddy's side he jogs.
"May I count them for you dad?
I'm the best counter you've ever had!"

8. *He importantly counts from the first to the last*
every hog that waddles past.
He reports that there are only nine,
"dad, I almost ran out of fingers that time!"

9. *He and dad are in the garden now,*
he wants to hoe and dad shows him how.
The hoe is heavy and the handle too long,
but daddy's helper struggles on.

10. *A trickle of sweat runs down his face*
and daddy says "let's take a break".
Dad must know what it is like
trying to be a man when you're just a tike.

11. *Dad is tinkering in the hood of the car,*
his little helper wants to know just what things are.
"What's that black hose dad, that metal box too?
I want to know so I can fix cars like you!"

12. *"I'll hold the light dad while you look down there,*
that bolt has got to be around here somewhere!"
Dad smiles and thinks what would he do,
without his little helper who is so true-blue.

13. *When the sun goes down and the animals are fed,*
a sleepy little man is tucked in bed.
He thinks of all his manly deeds
and all the help his daddy needs.

14. *"Good night daddy, I need to rest,*
so tomorrow I can work my best."
"Son, you make your daddy glad,
you're the best little helper I've ever had!"

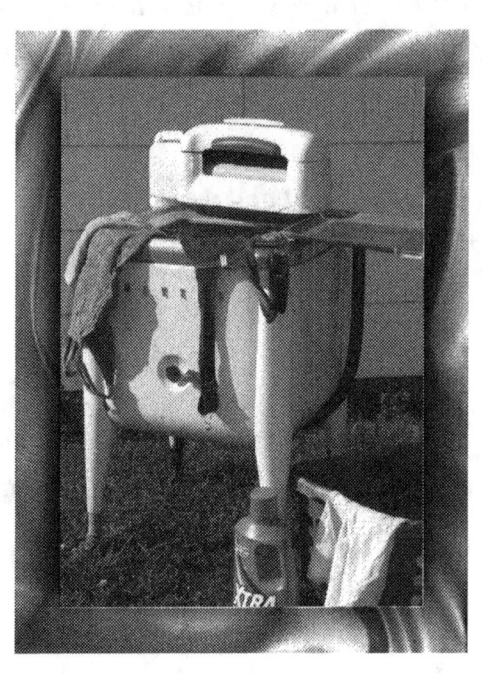

CHAPTER 6

Wisdom Wrung from the Wringer

The question of which piece of household equipment is most useful to an ordinary housewife is debatable; however in the case of a FARM housewife, the answer is much clearer. What could be more important, useful, and absolutely necessary than a wash machine? Especially if you have not 1, 2, or even 5 kids, but a near dozen?! Kids that ride horses and steers, kids that make mud pies, climb sappy pine trees, roast marshmallows, swim in mud puddles…. Do you begin to see the whole grimy picture?

My tale begins in the week of the big rainfall we had last month. Day after day without sunshine meant that the laundry pile didn't diminish any (the dryer just couldn't keep up with the mound) and under the circumstances (remember, it rained all week) it steadily grew taller. In the mornings after chores, 7 chore - kids and their dad shed 8 pairs of soaking jeans and eight pairs of soggy socks. In the evening after chores, 8 shirts were added to the pile and probably more socks. (It's a blessing that the two littlest kids and mom didn't get out-side enough to get dirty!)

As the days went by, overalls and coveralls were added to the pile and soon even the treasured "spares" perched grimly at the top, be –speckled and splashed. Just when the dresser drawers were looking bare, and the kitchen floor above the laundry pile appeared to be rising in an odd peak, the SUN came out! Oh how wonderful the warm rays felt on the face! It was a joy to be out in the warm breeze and golden sunlight. As you can imagine, mom got us busy right away on that mountainous laundry pile. After all, in Minnesota you can never predict the weather and the storm clouds might appear again at any minute. We all gathered 'round the pile and began sorting like wild! What a pile of socks! Such a mound of muddy tee-shirts! And my! The mountain of jeans beat all! We loaded up that old Maytag washer to the brim, poured on the detergent and let 'er go! Only....she didn't go. UH OH. No one could think of a thing to say, except Maggie who never loses her tongue. She yelled out our standard family distress call: "DAAAD!!"

Well, dad the fix-it-man looked the Maytag up and down, over, under and inside out but sadly informed us that our washing machine would be of use no longer. What a blow! Suddenly dad's face lit up in a grin. "Cheer up kids! I just happen to have a spare washer out in the garage!" In the garage? We didn't remember any washer in the ......wait a minute! Could that old tub on wheels with the strange revolving roller pos-sibly be a washing machine? It turned out that it was -only it wasn't an automatic.

That day we rolled it up to the house and put it to use. It must have come from an old farm sale or something and was probably meant to be a piece of antique décor but by golly, that thing still worked! At first, it was a novelty running clothes through the wringer and seeing the dirty water run out. We fought over who got to do it and practically ran out to the washer every time the buzzer announced that it was our turn to wring out a load. Dad said he would be on the look out for an affordable automatic and the next week went by with the fights still going on over wringing loads out. By the NEXT week the arguments had cooled considerably and by the end of the month, it just wasn't a thrill anymore. It seemed to take twice as long to do laundry. Under-wear got caught when they went through the roller and went round and round and round while you tried to extract them and pinched your fingers. The beads on one of my favorite shirts nearly got crushed and some of the buckles on the overalls got all twisted up. A bearing began to ooze oil and stained a bedspread and we had to wring it out by hand since it couldn't fit through the roller.

One night at supper time we all bombarded dad with the same question: "When are you going to get an automatic washing machine?" He just smiled and said that he was still looking for just the right one. There was no guarantee of when we would get one, so we just learned to live with that old wringer-washer and learned some valuable lessons in the process. We concluded that beauty is only skin deep and crushed beads sparkle more than whole ones do. We learned to try and try again until we succeeded; even if the underwear emerged from the depths of the revolving wringer in shreds. Also, we found that beauty is in the eye of the beholder and a blanket that has oil stains on one side can always be placed with the good side up and still be as warm as ever. The value of recycling water became very clear to us as we watered flowers with brown, red and blue water from the washing machine and we learned to work even harder as we ridded the flower beds of not only weeds, but lint as well.

We learned to think before we spoke, since the one who complained about wringing was the most liable to land the job. All of us began to realize that we shouldn't put off until tomorrow the things we should have done yesterday and even though it took a bit longer to do laundry with a wringer washer, the laundry pile sunk down and disappeared more quickly then ever before! Us kids found out that it takes less time to do a thing right than to explain why you did it wrong , so we learned to be very precise about wringing all the dirty water out of socks, to be careful not to mix red's and white's and to rinse out the washer after doing a load of manure covered chore clothes if we didn't want our Sunday best to smell and look of mysterious things. And in the end we realized that when you reverse the old saying "not everything that glitters is gold" to "not everything that is gold, glitters", it fit our old machine perfectly. With that dent in its side and that rusty lid and legs it certainly didn't glitter, but it WAS like gold since we learned so many valuable things from it! Folks must have been mighty good people back in the days they used wringer washers!!

Well my friends, this tale ends with a snappy looking Maytag washer sitting where the old one once sat and the wringer washer back in the garage. It's a little sad seeing that faithful old machine that rose to the occasion when we needed it, gathering dust in a far corner of the garage. You know what I'm going to do? I think I'll use that old wringer washer when I have kids just to teach them (like my dad did) some of those golden lessons that have almost been forgotten by our generation. We sure were lucky to be able to wring some wisdom from that old wringer.

◄═ CHAPTER 7 ═►
When City Meets Country

We often have relatives from the city out to the farm for visits. They usually enjoy their stay, but most times are quite contented to go on back to the city, and to what is *normal* to their way of life. They've had good laughs over our scanty phone books, and the way we exclaim over the amount of traffic on our dirt road increasing from two cars, to three cars. They've smiled over our tiny towns and stores, and our habit of leaving the keys in the car. But of course, we've also had ample opportunity to laugh back at them!

Chicken butchering time is always quite amusing when we have city guests. I think we do it just to provoke them! The way they eye us, and scowl at our "cruelty" when we check a chicken leg for plumpness is hilarious! And then the gasping and groaning over the butchering process itself! (Grin) Holding their stomachs over the plucking and turning white over the cutting up....... (I'm sorry, it just seems so humorous!) But funniest of all is the way they sniff hungrily at the frying chicken and look longingly at it but refuse to eat a single bite of that "poor bird." Of course nobody really minds, it just leaves more for us!

Then there's the case of stink bombs. Oh yes! Every farm has a well concealed nest of eggs that were missed on a hunt. And every farm kid knows that those putrid bombs (depending on how "ripe" they are) will go off without warning. An "experienced" veteran knows that an unusually light egg isn't a safe thing to approach, let alone hold in your hand! But of course, how could our unsuspecting guests know all that? I never will know how they locate those remote nests of rotten eggs. We always know when the deed is done though. You can smell them coming a mile away! Having no "farm savvy" dad to warn them about the dangers of "light" eggs, they have to learn the hard way. No one can say that a farm is lacking in amusements! The way some city folk's quake over leaving the front door unlocked at night is also quite amusing. Some have even gone so far as placing a kitchen chair under the doorknob! Obviously they aren't used to our quiet ways of life here in the country.

There is one trick that farm kids absolutely *can not* resist playing on their city friends and relatives. This is the old "pump the tail" trick. Some kids have absolutely no idea where milk comes from. The last thing they expect is for it to be squeezed out of the udder! So you can see why some of them would be extremely gullible when told that pumping the cow's tail makes the milk stream into the bucket. All you have to do is milk the cow and tell the innocent friend to "keep pumping!" "Faster! Faster!" They really believe it too! What you do to motivate them is to tell "Bossy" to make *chocolate milk!* You should see the way they pump then! Now don't get me wrong, there are those certain people who come from the freeways, high rise apartments, loud traffic and seem to fit right in here. They roll up their sleeves and dig into country life with a will! They'd fit in with the biggest bumpkins of us all! They are fun on hayrides, helpful with chores, (even butchering!) enjoy bike rides on country roads, wear the appropriate farm attire-I can see my male cousins looking into the mirror trying the effect of a bandana around their neck! Yes these people have got it down! It's funny how people change, especially kids who have been on the farm for a few weeks. They come out here looking pale and sickly with soft hands and feet. Back home again they go with hands full of slivers, a few scratches here, a bruised knee there, a nice suntan and a wish list for their mom and dad. "Can't we take just *one* goat home with us?" "Daddy, we could fit at least two rabbits in the trunk!"

I can remember the fun times spent with our city relatives sleeping out in the tent, having bonfires, harvesting sweet corn, swimming in the lake, picking strawberries, and just plain enjoying life. They realize what a gift it is that country people possess. Peace and quiet, friendly people in quaint little towns, fresh air, space for living, freedom; yes, that's what we're all about. And you know what? They come here just to get it. Sometimes we take our country surroundings for granted, out here where the pavement "ends" and the cornfields begin. No matter who our city visitors may be they still appreciate some of the precious things that we have. Even the ones who agonize over butchering procedures love the farm. They can marvel over the brightness of the stars at night, here where there are no city lights to dim them. City visitors, return home with memories of sweet apple cider, beautiful wild flowers, delicious homemade ice cream and warm baby kittens.

CHAPTER 8
Barn Dance

oesn't the phrase "barn dance" just set your mind whirling with all sorts of pleasant thoughts? Straw bales, cowboy boots, popcorn, whirling skirts, foot stompin' fiddle tunes, glowing lights.....ahh the whole works! A wholesome "country" way of having a good time! As we begin to make plans for our fourth barn dance, memories of the other three come back to me. I was quite young for all of them and it's been a while, but memories like those don't often dim. One change we have made in our barn dances is the "invitation only". The original sign at the end of our dirt road advertising, "Barn Dance 1/2 Mile" soon brought in every cowpoke (and a few other types) from miles around!

I remember the excitement of cleaning out the big Quonset. Dust blew up in plumes as we swept it out, and afterwards dad carefully sprinkled flax seed on the floor for the dancers. I thought the straw bale "bleachers" dad constructed to line the walls, were the neatest things in the world! Machinery was driven out and parked somewhere else to make room for the "stage" (a trailer flatbed). Yes, we had live entertainment! Our feature performers for one year were "The Maras Sisters and Jacob" and local talent performed in-between. What a variety of talent that was! There were country singers, fiddlers, guitarists, keyboard, accordion, harmonica and concertina players.....the list goes on!

As it was an authentic farm-yard atmosphere, it was pertinent that we pen up the sheep and post "DANGER-WILD BULL" signs about. And of course there is nothing more "authentic" country than a rustic out-house. You can smile all you want, but doesn't that fit in right well with a barn dance? Our invitations (when we used them) stated: "Out-house provided!" There was even a moon carved in the side! However, we did experience a bit of trouble with that out-house. Some mischievous youngin's decided to have some fun, and later when a few little ones were found to be missing, they were discovered locked inside! (By the way, we've eliminated the outer latch and have since modernized to a spring for keeping the door from blowing in the wind!)

One barn dance comes back to me particularly well. We had planned it for my mom's East Coast brother. The only problem was, when barn dance time came, no one could wake him up! He had spent the previous two weeks in Italy, flown home to Maryland, left the next day for Minnesota and drove for two days arriving just in time for the dance! No wonder he wasn't in the mood for partying!

The details of another dance are still fresh in my mind. When the big night finally arrived there was much excitement! I was very eager to put on my western skirt and blouse for the big occasion! Mom lit two glowing torches for the end of the driveway and soon cars, vans and trucks began rolling in. Vehicles lined the driveway three rows deep, and the whole back yard was full also. (The youngsters found out after dark that the "parking lot" was a great place to play hide-and-seek.) It seemed like the cars never stopped coming, but the music didn't wait! It filled the night, inviting dancers to come on in and have fun! Light poured from the huge double door way of the Quonset and spilled out into the darkness. Inside, the soft light from overhead bulbs glinted on shiny boots and buckles, and the whirling skirts were mesmerizing if you stared at them too long! The air was filled with the scent of warm popcorn from the stand in the corner and a festive checkered cloth covered the table spread with potluck "goodies". Those who didn't dance or were taking a break, sat on the bleachers visiting or just watching the couples.

The young children like myself would, from time to time, venture out into the night for a couple games of "Red Rover", "Kick the Can" or Hide-and-Seek", but nothing was as interesting as watching the couples on the dance floor. Round and round they would go, now to a sad waltz, now to a romping polka or a jazzy country swing dance. Mom took the stage to sing her traditional "Mamma's Don't Let Your Babies Grow up To Be Cowboys" and received an encore with boot stomping and hand slapping.

As I mentioned before, our barn dance definitely had an authentic country atmosphere. Later in the evening the guests got to experience this first hand when the entire sheep herd ran onto the dance floor! Uh-oh! Some little cowboy wanted to play stampede I guess, and left the pen open. There was a roundup of sorts and the sheep were soon penned up securely, but yet another mishap was in store. In the middle of a lively fiddle tune the power suddenly went out! Complete blackness covered the crowd, but I'll tell you what, those country fiddlers just kept on making music until power was restored again! And when much later the bleachers were full of sleeping babies and tired out dancers, it was time for everyone to hit the dusty trail. I was sad to see it end, but those memories are cause for much anticipation with our upcoming barn dance. It's been a long time. Too long. The fellowship, atmosphere and good old-fashioned fun of a barn dance can't be found anywhere else!

CHAPTER 9
Ready- Set- STUCCO!

There are times in our human existence when we are faced with huge obstacles. Obstacles that give cause for a dry mouth, clammy hands and weak knees. I stood, a mere 5 ft. 4in. creature, gazing up at the 30ft. monstrosity, suffering all the aforementioned symptoms. Boy, that house seemed big! Was it humanly possible to circle it three times, each time plastering on a layer of stucco? THREE times! I shuddered. Well, the summer stretched before us and even if it took us all twelve weeks, I knew we would do it somehow, because that's the way we are. After the initial shock of the size of the obstacle/job, I took care not to look at the entire thing in all its awfulness, but instead focused on just little pieces.

The day dawned when we were to begin, and the first part of the job was to remove the worn, pressed board siding. The Asian beetles weren't too happy about evacuating their comfortable residence, but it was that or be smothered under stucco. Our

house, bared of its pressed siding, revealed an antique- looking covering of cedar siding, yellowed paint and dust of bygone years. Now that the job had actually begun, we
threw ourselves into it with all our young energy. It took only a day or so to remove the
pressed siding, and perhaps another couple days to staple wire over the cedar siding. We
looked up at that house with a sense of satisfaction that we had done well thus far-but
the most difficult phase of the job was yet to come.

I never realized how heavy a bag of cement could be (I couldn't lift it off the ground),
how sore an arm can become when wielding a cement trowel and how hot a Minnesota summer can be! (Somehow we chose the hottest part of summer to stucco our
house!) We labeled the four sides of the house, north, south, east, and west and began
to laboriously make our way around it, somewhat like ants frosting a gigantic cake.
However, stucco isn't as pliable as frosting, and it doesn't taste nearly as good. I know,
because I've let my mouth open one too many times under a drippy trowel. I thought
that the hardened droplets of cement on the top of my head would cause my hair to
dry up and crack off in places, and that my lime-dehydrated hands would never be
smooth again. But of course it wasn't as bad as that.

We worked in the cool morning hours and always tried to finish a wall before the
sun would come creeping along and beat us, swallowing every inch of shade. Stuc-
coing, like any physical work, requires lot's of energy and of course to have energy,
one must eat accordingly. Oh how we looked forward to dinnertime! What might
it be today? Pizza? Pasta and clams? Scalloped potatoes and ham? Chicken soup or
hamburgers? (We really got special treatment during our labors!) Maybe there will be
brownies or apple pie for dessert! Ears perked up at the sound of pots banging around
in the kitchen and we sniffed hungrily from outside the window at delectable aromas-
sometimes identifiable, sometimes not.

One day, we were on the second layer I believe, I discovered that heights don't
agree with me. Dad was mixing cement and we were in a hurry on the south side,
so I volunteered to go up to the top with my brother in the scaffolding. Bad mistake
- I couldn't move! I thought maybe all the stucco I had swallowed was finally taking
its toll and had solidified in my joints, but that was not so. The truth was I was fright-
fully and fearfully afraid of heights. I tried to laugh at how silly I was being but it was

no good I tell you. Silly or not, things were looking serious. Breakfast was nearing the surface. Involuntarily, two salty tears dribbled down my face creating furrows in the dusty lime that adorned my cheeks and I didn't have to look in a mirror to know that my face was gray. There I stood, shaking in my boots and dropping tears from the end of my nose. Dad looked up at me and said, "are you sure you're the same girl who wanted to go to Valley Fair this summer?" They got me down somehow and the world began to look bright again. It turns out that I got a brand-new job too! I was demoted...er...promoted to cement mixer, wheel-barrel toter and low-down (as in near the ground) stucco girl.

Round and round we went gaining confidence, speed AND muscle as we went along. When the heat became oppressive, the arms tired and the hour for dinner was far, we sang. All of our favorite harmonizing tunes filled the air renewing our energy and filling us with joy. Then came that grand day when we were to complete the very last layer of stucco on the very last wall. It was the west wall which had the most open surface to cover. We were at it early in the morning, expecting it to take nearly all day. Everyone was pretty enthusiastic and we worked amazingly fast. When coating a wall for the last time there must be no pausing because otherwise a seam will show up when one segment dries before the other. We mentally broke the wall into four segments and applied stucco from top to bottom as quickly as we could, blending them together. Dad had invented a pattern for the final coat earlier on and we each tried our best to duplicate the sweeping, random curves. (Our house testifies to the fact that we each have our own unique style...)

2:30 pm that day marked the end of a job that miraculously was completed in 1 and ½ weeks. We were so proud of our handiwork, the strong, grayish white structure with its unique patterns appeared invincible to any stormy blast. When the trim was painted white it looked even grander! Every minute of labor was infinitely worth it-there is nothing like looking back on a job well done-and an obstacle conquered.

CHAPTER 10
Rodeo Time!

he wooden bleachers aren't exactly comfortable, but I wouldn't trade this seat for anything. The cool evening breeze blows across the crowd bringing with it the scent of hay, horses, dust and popcorn. I know I couldn't possibly eat popcorn now; I need my hands for clapping and my mouth for screaming 'cause it's RODEO TIME!!

Excitement begins to mount as we see cowboys hanging around the bucking chutes testing the special saddles, wrapping their wrists and securing chaps. I can hardly contain myself because you see, rodeo is my favorite sport! There is something so realistic about Rodeo. The livestock, the dust, the battered cowboy hats and scuffy boots. It's the knowledge that if something doesn't go right, it could mean life or death. It's the bravery and daring of each and every roper and rider, gambling his life and money in a sport that's not only a game but a way of life.

A hush falls over the crowd as a girl in glittering costume riding a beautiful horse gallops into the arena holding the American flag. She halts in the center and her horse prances as the flag waves proudly on the breeze. We rise as one with beating hearts as our National Anthem throbs over the sound system and echoes off the grand stand. A second or two of perfect silence when it is finished and then the crowd erupts into wild cheering-it's show time!

These high-heeled cowboy boots are pinching my toes a bit but you just don't attend a rodeo in tennis shoes. The man in front of me is blocking my vision with a monstrous white Stetson, but I won't let him spoil my fun. I prop my chin on my palm and lean around him. The fun is about to begin folks, and with one of my favorite events: bare-back bronc riding! The crowd is roaring as one after another, wiry young cowboys plunge out of the chutes on wildly kicking and bucking horses! My body is tense and a breath of restricted air escapes my lungs after every ride. There is no pause in the excitement and soon we see the cowboys riding saddle on the broncs. As they twist and plunge through the air I imagine these "out-law" horses galloping across the open range, untamed and untouched by man. Now it is ropers and steer wrestlers who take the stage. Music pounds from the speakers and the cowboys seem to keep perfect time as they toss their ropes or dive off of their horses to test their strength against muscular, long horned steers. Every minute I expect someone to be injured, but so far I've only seen a few limps.

Being the person I am, I can't keep myself from feeling along with the cowboys, their occasional losses. Maybe it's a fall from a bronc long before the bell, perhaps a run-away steer he never even got a loop around or one that refused to be conquered in a wrestling match. I see the droop in his shoulders as the crowd gives a disappointed "oooohhh...", and the way he tries to keep his head high as he scoops up a bent up cowboy hat and walks...or limps... out of the arena. The crowd goes wild over the next act, but my eyes follow the form of the forlorn cowboy as he climbs up on the chutes next to his buddies. They thump him encouragingly on the back, but I realize that that cowboy probably lost a lot more than we'll ever know.

I am jolted out of my reverie. The rodeo announcer in his rich baritone has just announced something that made the crowds go wild and I soon join the cheering when

I realize what it's for. The ladies are barrel racing! With faces full of determination, they gallop one after another into the arena tightly turning around the three barrels. After a colorful flash of mane, tail, and western blouse, they're gone, leaving a trail of dust and a breathless audience waiting eagerly for the score. I like this part of the rodeo particularly because of how many beautiful horses you get to see, all with their unique colorings and markings. All too soon it is over- but the best is yet to come!

Over the loud speaker come the words everyone has been waiting to hear: "Who's ready for some BULL RIDING?!" Of course we're ready and we let him know! This is my favorite part, but it doesn't stop me from holding my breath for the cowboys. Charging out of chute 1 is a huge spotted bull with a great big Brahma lump. What a twister! He spins around the arena like crazy. That cowboy doesn't stay seated for long. Chute 2 ejects a dark Brahma who would snort fire if he could. What a character! He's a twister, crow-hopper, bucker and charger all in one! We are all amazed at the strength and stamina of this cowboy for he makes the bell. The rodeo clowns are in action, distracting the bull with their funny antics and bright clothing. Whoa! One of them just got a ride on that Brahma's horns! Chutes 3 and 4 contain bulls just as mean, and once the cowboys have fallen off they must literally run for their lives!

Oh the excitement! I totally ignore the pinching of my toes and thank goodness that the guy in front of me took down that Stetson to let the breeze cool his perspiring bald top. He is only a "wanna be" cowboy by the looks of the brand new Nike's and flaming Hawaiian print shirt. I guess he thought the Stetson was enough to make him look the part.Out of Chute 6 dives the final bull and his rider. The audience seems to cease breathing altogether or perhaps it's just the blaring music that covers it up. We gape in amazement as this bull charges into the middle of the arena and makes a dead stop shooting his rider high into the air. That was a quick ride!

The grand-stand erupts into a cheering, waving mass of happy faces as the cheerful melody of "Happy Trails" fills the night air. It ended all too soon for me! I think of all of those cowboys and cowgirls headed for another arena in another place to ride for another crowd. Rodeo is a way of life, a job, a gamble and a sport. One of the very best. Happy trails folks!

CHAPTER 11
Disaster in the Parlor

It was disaster alright, but not in a comfortable decorative parlor, oh no. Instead, disaster in the form of Bernadette the cow, and her accomplice Bonnie Bell, struck in a smelly *milk* parlor on a muggy September night. It happened that the men of the family were away for the day, and called to say that they were going to be home a bit late. That meant only one thing to us girls, the milking must commence without them. It was perfectly logical too, that groans were the only conversation on the way out to the barn. The reason? Well for one thing, Bernadette and I are enemies because of a past conflict. (Nothing more than she kicking me over twice into the manure and filling my rubbers with milk) Secondly, the 1955 surge milker that the boys used was rather a mystery to us. The machine was new technology for our family and dad had set it up so that chores would go quicker for the school year. Truthfully the machine didn't always make things easier. Sometimes, as in this case, it did just the opposite.

Our chores consisted of taking care of the other animals on the farm like chickens, rabbits, pigs, sheep and such. And because of this, we were quite uncertain as to how the two mischievous cows would behave for us- not to mention the milk machine. Proven in our minds, was the fact that the two milk cows preferred male company. If ever there was a set of women haters it was those two. Bernadette herself had proved that, when she swiped me off my brothers milking stool. Nonetheless we led Bonnie Bell and Bernadette into the parlor, for what else could we do? We did know that my brother put the milker on Bonnie Bell while he milked Bernadette by hand so as to get two done at once. I felt a million times safer crawling under Bonnie Bell (jumpy as she was) to hook up the milker, than I did sitting on a stool anywhere near Bernadette. Therefore, I volunteered my sister to milk the ornery cow. After all, she liked her better than me.

We plugged in the generator to start the suction, then slung the harness over Bonnie's back. I leaned over and tried to hook the 25 pound stainless steel bucket to the metal hook under the cow's belly. It swayed a bit, then crashed to the ground, screeching against the cement floor. Bonnie jumped from the din and stomped a heavy foot down on the suction hose. Running around to one side we desperately tried to get her foot of the hose before she severed it. Stubborn animal! Not one foot would she budge. In frustration my sister rammed against her leg and she hopped backward off of our hose. Hands on my hips I blew a strand of hair out of my eyes and squatted down beside the milk machine. Four pairs of hands reached under the cow and lifted the bucket into place. Thwack! (I wonder if all cows have a mean streak........) She sure knew when we were helpless and took advantage of it. Swinging her thick tail, Bonnie Bell slapped us repeatedly in the face. It's rather hard to hook up a heavy milking machine when you can't see for cow hair stinging in your eyes, but within a few minutes it was attached and we crawled to safety away from that cow, only to face another twice as bad!

From the beginning she had the advantage. Bernadette knew we were timid around her without dad there, and the way she flaunted her tail made me angry. As soon as my sister sat down to milk, she scooted way over to the wall and planted her feet firmly on the cement. Oh! That smug look! Well that didn't stop us. Francesca climbed up on the bunk and rammed against Bernadette's side trying to get her to move over. No go. That lousy cow just kept munching corn with an air of complacency that would make one sick! Francesca was smart though. An unsuspected jab in the ribs brought Bernadette to her senses (for the time being) and she stepped back into her place hurriedly. I held onto the tail to keep it from slapping Francesca while she sat down once again to have a try.

Bernie wasn't about to be beat by a bunch of girls. After a few squirts, out flashed her leg, missing Francesca by inches. Was I ever mad then! Glaring at that.......... cow, I wiped a trickle of sweat off my cheek and twisted her tail tighter than ever. Just when I was about to twist her tail off, she was saved by the milk machine. My sisters and I jumped at the awful sucking, gurgling sound of the suction cups sliding off the udder of the calm Bonnie Bell. Once again squatting on either side of her, we spent more time in the humid parlor, trying to put it back on her. The few flies in the room seemed to know exactly when our hands weren't free, and buzzed incessantly around our face and arms. Looking at each others streaked and beet red faces caused us to burst out laughing, but this merriment was short lived. *Smack* went Bernadette's tail on Francesca's face as she sat down. I reached for her tail and missed as once again she scooted over to the wall and remained rigid and stubborn. The room seemed to be getting hotter by the minute. Every time Francesca got close enough to Bernie to actually milk, the naughty cow would take a step or two in a different direction.

Suddenly, we had a brilliant idea. I remembered that my brother always sang songs to the cows while he milked them. Perhaps that was the problem. Maybe the secret of milking those two, was to sing to them! At this idea we commenced to sing some of our favorite tunes with new energy. At the same time, Francesca cautiously leaned closer to Bernadette reaching out her arms in an attempt to finish the milking job. Whoosh! Man that animal was fast on her feet! Francesca leaped out of the way and frowned at us music makers. It dawned on us rather suddenly that maybe the cows didn't like the soprano sound. Perhaps it was my brother's baritone they were partial to. Alright, a few low notes weren't going to get in our way! Accordingly, the three of us that weren't milking cleared our throats and sang the very best baritone that we could manage. I found that looking down at the floor and bending the knees a little produced a deeper sounding effect. (More like a sick bull than anything else!)

Just when I thought that we had found the secret, Bernadette's ears flattened and she prepared for another kick. I gave up straining my throat on low notes, in exasperation. "I've got it!" One of the twins exclaimed all of a sudden. "It's the *style* of music that's bothering her!" "I think Clayton sings her polkas!" *Style of music, my foot*, I thought darkly. If that was the case, this spoiled animal needed some discipline! What else could we do though? The job needed to be done. (Although I must admit, the delightfully wicked thought occurred to me to let Bernadette suffer with her full udder all night, since she didn't want us to milk her.) "We might as well give it a try." I said looking out into the dark night. "It's getting pretty late." Sounding something like a rusty tuba ensemble, we squeaked through the refrain of the "Too Fat" polka, aiming the words right at my plump foe while still struggling to maintain a "masculine" pitch. My patience was already worn threadbare, when Bernadette, casting the last straw, showed her contempt for us by plopping a fresh cow patty on the parlor floor. It's a good thing that the guys drove in at that moment, because visions of grilled steak and cheeseburgers were swimming before my eyes as I glared at that detestable animal.

You have never seen the likes of how Bernadette acted when Clayton came into the parlor to relieve us. Back in her proper place, she was munching corn, and innocently swinging that wretched tail. Clayton sat down on the milking stool and she looked back at him sweetly with those big brown eyes. Argh! Would you believe it?! I walked out of the parlor patting Bonnie Bell on the back for being half way decent, and snubbed Bernadette completely.

CHAPTER 12
Farm Life: The Real Life

he hum of corn dryers and combines, the beautiful fall colors, the rumble of semi's and plumes of dust…it's all part of the harvest season. Row by row the crops disappear unbelievably fast as the days go by. Soon our little farm will be surrounded only by acres and acres of bare ground, a bleak contrast to the golden and brown that fills them now. It's all part of the cycle of life though. Round and round we go, planting, producing, harvesting and then beginning all over again. That is what life is all about.

On my return home recently from a visit out East, I truly began to appreciate the sense of reality that is found in the country. Somehow the multiple lanes, smokestacks, racing lights, crowded streets and strange faces are all whirled together into something that is completely foreign to "real life". The continuous cycle that is so easily discovered out here among the corn fields and gravel roads, is out there in the city, lost somewhere amidst the confusion. I'm glad to be back!

It's nice to peek in on my little guinea chicks and see how they've grown since I was gone. It's wonderful to feed the dogs right out of my hand and feel their warm tongues against my palm. How lovely it is to see the sun rise in the east without obstructing sky scrapers ruining the effect of purple and pink layered clouds. The familiar scent of hay bales, grass, and pine trees is so welcome after the fumes of the city. And the miles upon miles of open land lend a freedom to the soul that is rarely found. I'm back to reality; the reality of working with the land, the reality of new life, growth and death.

During the fall you will find us working quite a bit with the land. The planting and growing season is over and just like the farmers in the field we gather the work of our hands. Tomato's, peppers onions, potatoes, squash, carrots, apples and many other vegetables and fruits are gathered in and preserved. The Lord has been good to us and there is something so "real" about working with the land He gave us as a gift. We tended it, nurtured it, planted in it, took from it and now we tend it again preparing it for a well deserved rest. The earth will lie dormant until spring breezes blow and we stir it up again for the planting season.

There is always new life on the farm and besides my little guinea chicks, there are two batches of kittens in the hayloft. Mom is none too happy about these newest members of the farmyard, but the kids are overjoyed! It's beyond me how a cat can birth and raise a batch of kittens and then have a whole new batch in 3 months-but that's another story! Our annual fall measurement day took place with many new marks on the wall telling a tale of growth. That is excepting the one mark that stayed put. Everybody's mark went up but mine. (Sigh…) But the kids aren't the only ones growing! My little Bantam hens are finally grown up and are beginning to lay after 6 months. The six little calves are hardly little anymore. The kids fed them milk as long as possible (I think there was a sort of contest on whose calve would get the largest the quickest) but finally I believe they have graduated to just feed and water. Jake the new puppy has grown so much since August that it's unbelievable! He is beginning to loose his pudgy puppy look. How fast time flies! And as far as growth goes… I think that's all…wait! Bernadette the cow has grown decidedly fatter. Hamburger?

And farm life wouldn't be reality at all if there was not death. Lately none of the kids have had any reason to lament of a pet rabbit but there recently was a "death" that on one felt too badly about. This being the butchering of the mean old bull who is now safely packaged into the freezer where he belongs. Cute little piglets have grown up into fat finished hogs and have been shipped of to market. And in about a month the sheep herd will loose many of its heaviest lambs.

There is peacefulness in being so close to the simple cycles and changes of life. They are all around us, but I believe they are never so clear and realistic as they are on the farm and out in the country.

CHAPTER 13
The Plentiful Vegetable Woes

Now is the time when Mother Earth opens wide,
the arms in which her treasures hide.
An abundance of good things to eat are now here,
We gather them in for the cold months so near.
Among all these treasures that we are enjoying,
There are a few whose abundance there is NO surpassing.

2. The apple so rosy and healthy they say,
Eat one a day and keep the doctor away
If that saying is true I'll be healthy indeed
At the rate I've been eating no doc will I need!
Apples from sunup right to sundown
I'm all set to be fit from my toes to my crown.

3. Mom has been busy and it's amazing to find
In how many dishes an apple may hide.

The sauce we had for breakfast, the fresh slices at lunch,
I bet there'll be apple crisp for supper and cake for tomorrow's brunch.
It's rather shocking how tired of apple pie one can be,
But the tongue is a finicky thing you see.

4. I'm afraid that the case just stated above,
Is the very same with the zucchini I used to love.
The first glimpse of green squash is a sight to behold,
But after all these months the flavor gets old.

5. Zucchini fried was my favorite style,
But the Italian Frittata took its place after a while.
Baked with filling wasn't really the best,
And when stewed with tomatoes it just lost its zest!
Boiled zucchini filled the house with its smell,
And sautéed with garlic did the same as well.

6. As the plants got bigger our faces became green,
But when it comes to hiding zucchini, my mom is the queen.
The pancakes she served for breakfast were an unmistakable green,
Not to mention the bread that had a zucchini plants sheen.
But the cream cheese frosting on that cake couldn't hide,
The little green shreds we spotted inside.
And although like dutiful children we got the dishes down,
I'm elated to see the troublesome plant become brown.

7. Now I speak of the fair Elderberry not very well known,
In our very own orchard many are grown.
The tiny purple berries will stain just like ink,
And the concoction mom makes I could pour down the sink.
If ever you have a sniffle, tickle or cough,

Don't let mom know about it, just laugh it off!
For if you don't she will soon make you take,
So many healthy elderberries, your tummy will ache.
A sniffle or cough is better by far,
than taking purple elderberries straight from the jar.

8. *No sooner did we get over the zucchini plants green,*
when mom was filling our plates with the tasty string bean.
We canned jar after jar but it's a sin to waste,
After meals and meals of beans will we ever forget the taste?
The beans just kept on coming; we picked them every week,
We thought there were a lot at the beginning, but found more during their peak!

9. *Green bean salad and green bean soup,*
Green bean pasta and green bean goop!
We ate them raw, we ate them whole,
We ate them with our meat and in casserole.
And when the green in our faces finally began to fade,
It was time to dig potatoes with shovel and spade.

10. *Buttery mashed potatoes are good truth be told,*
and for many a day they didn't get old.
Baked potatoes were great with lots of sour cream,
And the potato soup mom made was just like a dream!
Even dad manned the oven, potatoes are his style,
We weren't tired of hash browns for quite a long while.

11. *French Fries at McDonald's are good you know,*
But much better are the ones made with potatoes you grow.
A breakfast of thick potato pancakes they say,
Will make you work like a man for the rest of the day.

We sure hoped that was true 'cause the food in our hatch,
Was all burned up before noon digging in that huge potato patch.
But by the time each potato dish had been served once or twice,
We decided it was better to get our starch through rice.

12. Perhaps of these all, the onion is best,
At sneaking its way into dishes you liked best.
The buckets on our porch bleakly speak
Of months of onions, of weeks and weeks!
And if I am honest, the truth will I say,
I dislike onions in the very worst way!

13. When a bite of home-made pizza has an unusual sting
I know which vegetable mom is secretly using.
The beef soup is flavored with onions of course,
But sliced on a burger they are considerably worse.
At the smell of onions and liver my stomach does flips,
But supper looks no better with chicken and onion strips.
The tomato salad I never liked anyway,
Would probably, without the onions, be better any day!

14. Yet the truth must be told, we must not blame the cook,
What else can she do with vegetables that fill every nook?
And when the snow flies I'm sure we will pine,
for the flavorful fruits and veggies once in their prime.
For the salads and pies, pancakes and bread,
And all the things we now seem to dread.

(And now that I am through with this long tale of woe,
Back to the steaming canner I go!)

CHAPTER 14

Canning—Well Worth the Effort

Canning season is a busy time of year for gardeners in SW Minnesota and all across the country. Gardening, like anything else has its seasons, and stages. In the spring, of course, it's planting seeds and small plants, and then on to summer with watering, weeding, weeding, and more weeding. And with fall comes the joy of harvesting the fruits of your labor, and canning them. *Canning them?!* That's where we're at now friends! Rows of Kerr and Ball jars sit serenely on our basement shelf, displaying lovely fruits and vegetables and shining prettily. But oh, if they could tell a story! Those of you who still can garden produce, and those of you who used to, know what I mean.

Canning season is: Wakeup call at the ungodly hour of 6 a.m. "Time to get up Kids!" (Groan, roll over) "Hurry up!" (Sit up in bed) "We've got lots of canning to do!" (Fall flat on back again)We're out in the garden picking tomatoes, grapes, cucumbers, carrots, and beans to fill the overwhelming amount of empty glass jars ready and waiting on the kitchen counter. The idea was to get up early and beat the hungry mosquitoes, but evidently they're on to us. Back in the house again with baskets of produce and huge appetites.

What's for breakfast? Toast. Toast?! With Jelly? Please.......? Ok. (During canning season, quick breakfasts are a necessity) After wiping the sticky spots off of the tile floor and getting rid of crumbs, the glass jars once again loom before us. We begin to snap beans. Somebody's not so good at hitting the bucket. The mound of bean-ends surrounding us gets taller, as we try to get the job done fast. The juicer is bubbling on the stove, and mom is washing cucumbers at the sink. I am commissioned to make the pickle brine. Mrs. Wages must have been one tough woman, I think, as my eyes water over the steaming vinegar. After putting her little packet of pre-mixed powder into the vinegar-water mixture, I for one, can't take the smell and sting! I'm out on the porch with streaming eyes after vainly trying to cover them with one hand and stir with the other. Did I ever like dills?

Bean snapping has commenced and we're on to washing carrots. It seems like we never can avoid an accident during this important season, and before long, someone knocks a full half gallon glass jar of milk off the counter. Glass shatters in every direction and milk sprays everything! *Man*! Why did that have to happen *now?!* Making herself heard above the din, mom orders everyone to vacate the kitchen. Then she and I, take an hour off from canning, and spend it mopping under the refrigerator, stove and table, and getting glass splinters out of our fingers. No, we mustn't give up on canning yet! A few hours after that, behold- (oh glorious!) rows of green beans in sparkling glass jars on the counter. The pride in seeing part of our job well done, spurs us onward with new energy!

Now we fill waiting jars with lovely purple grape concentrate from the juicer. We are progressing quite well but after a few drips here and a few drips there, somebody steps unknowingly in the little purple puddles. Honestly, it looks as if a purple intruder has left his ghastly purple footprints behind him in a tour of our kitchen. From counter to table from stove to sink and back again they go, and the green bean ends sticking to them doesn't really improve the situation. No matter, the milk episode was much worse. As we go about our canning, there is an unmistakable odor coming up from the basement and surrounding us. Yes, dad's at it again. He's brewing up a storm of Sauer kraut down there, and don't we know it. It's in the middle of its fermenting process and stronger than ever. That too, will soon be put into jars and canned.

Uh oh! As mom carefully removes a jar of tomatoes out of the canner, it blows up mingling red with the already purple and green kitchen! The spattered cupboards, with red tomato sauce dribbling slowly down their fronts, look as though they've committed murder. Mom sets her lips, and once more the kitchen is vacated. Before long the discouraging mess has diminished reasonably. The purple footprint culprit has changed socks, green bean ends are whisked away in the dust pan, and the cupboards and counters have resumed their normal color. Since the eating area is still occupied with produce and jars, we settle for peanut butter and jelly sandwiches for supper.

What a long day! (Especially when lived on toast!) Despite all of the little problems we had, there is an overall feeling of satisfaction. Working together as a family we finished the job! Of course, there are many more days of canning left, (to live through) but when I look ahead to those cold winter days when we will all sit down and enjoy the fruits of our labors, canning season doesn't seem so bad!

CHAPTER 15
An Old Farmer

The harvest season reminds us just how fast time flies by. Planting, growing, harvesting and resting the soil, we go around and around. For many, there is hardly a moment of peace and quiet until all the crops are gathered in and the big job of harvesting complete. Yet in some places and in certain people there is a sort of silence, perhaps a wall separating past and present, a peaceful wandering over old dirt roads, amber fields and through cobwebby barns.

He sits there at the window trying to lift his tired old head to see out into the courtyard. Somehow I don't believe that the high brick wall, scrubby maple tree and drab bird house are what he's looking for, or even what he's seeing right now. At the moment he's far away from here, probably out on those 160 acres of what he calls: "de best black dirt ya'ver seen!" I've noticed him here several times before and have rather gotten into the habit of looking for him in the small group we play music for. Rarely does he seem to divert his gaze from the window and I hardly know if he realizes we are here. Once he surprised us by looking our way with an interested gaze when he heard the strains of that old melody, "Red River Valley".

There is a stamp upon him that set's him apart. The furrowed face cut by rain, snow and sleet, burnt by sun, wrinkled with care. Those great, big hands scarred with work, gentled with nursing and consecrated by the earth. The sparse frame broadened and bowed in the shoulders; that thrust of perseverance to his chin-they are all a mark of what he once was and what he will always be: a farmer. It seems to me that he doesn't belong here, rather like a rugged corn stalk in a hot-house. Ever since he came, he insisted on wearing those faded overalls. I know they mustn't be the most comfortable attire for someone bound to a wheel chair, but you see, those old overalls are a strong tie from the past. He still wipes grease from the old plow on them, scribbles figures and weights on the legs and fills the pockets with tid-bits just as imaginary for "de ode hosses, Jack 'n Abe".

He's tried to rise from that confining chair many times, gruffly explaining to anyone who will listen that "der are cows to be milked" and that "da ode sow in de back o' de shedtt" needs tending, but he's never more restless than in the fall. Just as you and I do, he must feel a change in the air and knows instinctively that now is the time when the ears are plump and full and the pods are ready to burst. He knows that he must tend to the fields before the cold winter winds arrive. The golden harvest moon rising magnificently over the brick wall calls to him, the lonely moan of the wind beckons him, the falling leaves of the Maple scurry to the ground urging him to hurry too.

He's sat the seat of a WD Alice Chalmers tractor, an Oliver 77, and an International M, pleasing all of the dealers with his variety of choices, but these days he just shouts to the horses he used to farm with when he was young. "Gidd-up ode Abe! Step up der Jack!" With closed eyes he once again makes the rounds on his quarter section seated on the corn binder with the lines in his capable hands.

He sits bowed in his chair reliving the poignant memories of autumns and harvests of the past. The smell of corn leaves and wood smoke in the air, the brilliant leaves of the orchard frosted silver every morning. The sound made by ears of corn hitting the bang board, wild, lonesome calls of the geese and ducks in a blue November sky, and pheasants bursting from a straw mound when approached. Ma's warm apple pie with that golden crust made with lard, homemade wine, freshly cured bacon and hams, apple cider, and rich black coffee. Threshing time, the roar of the machine, dust and chaff, the sweat of the horses and the clang of the bell announcing dinner and a home-made beer to the crew. Filling up the water heater on the cow tank with a bucket of cobs and watching fat hogs greedily gobble up ear corn. Running his fingers through the deep, thick winter coat of the horses and warming his hands over the woodstove or on the underside of the cow's udder on a chilly morning. Watching his young children play about the yard or help with the harvesting, knowing the importance they felt in being part of the effort. Seeing them grow up, his sons into young men of strength, his daughters into young ladies.

Why is there a pain in my young heart when I think ahead to the time when he will be reunited with the earth he loves so well. I can hardly bear to think of an empty wheel chair and a discarded pair of faded overalls. I can't think ahead to that time when the harvest moon may rise above the brick wall without the keen eye of the farmer watching its ascent. But this is just the un-fairness of youth that shrinks so from the Lord's Harvest. The old farmer will go on one day in the Lord's time, to Jack and Abe and take them on their rounds over that brand new 160 acre plot of "de best black dirt ya' ver seen!"

CHAPTER 16
The Midnight Marauder

Wanted: Mink Marauder-Dead or Alive

1. *Whispering through the treetops and swirling to the ground,*
The nighttime breeze was playing and the moon was
glowing down.
Almost every path was illumined, nearly every corner bright,
But unknowingly the moon, hid a small den out of sight.

2. *Soon all was nearly silent; the animals were all abed,*
The sheep were softly bleating and pony gently nodded her head.
Pleasant dreams of breakfast filled the minds of all the goats;
How they wheezed and chuckled over alfalfa and oats.

3. *The cows had delightful visions of how their stomachs*
would grow,
when breakfast was announced by the old red roosters crow.

Alas, if they but knew what terrible tidings morning would bring,
They would have given many breakfast's just to hear the rooster sing.

4. *But back in the woods from the darkened hole,*
A long dark creature silently stole.
A ray of moonlight slipping down from the sky
caught the face of the marauder, sinister and sly.
She padded along smooth and free,
Her rippling brown coat in the starlight you could see.

5. *From tree to tree, over twig and leaf,*
glided the mink, a predator and thief.
Alas! I ask of you my friends,
Why did she crave ours, instead of some other farmer's hens?
But she was not to be stopped; the chance was too good to pass by,
Her appetite was already whetted by a duck taken on the sly.

6. *And in but a minute her silent journey she had done,*
What an awful deed would happen before the rising of the sun.
The mink lifted up her face to the shelter of her prey,
The moon shone down on the henhouse making night as bright as day.

7. *She searched about, a lock was undone,*
Where was the farmer, where was the gun?!
Oh you evil mink, you need not go and hide,
He is asleep in bed while your victims snore inside.

8. *A squeeze later and she was in,*
the fat bitty's inside caused her to grin.
Clucking contentedly from each roost and nest,
Was the very meal a mink loves best

9. *Well let me tell you folks, the feathers flew,*
And sleeping in bed we never knew.
It must have been quite an extraordinary dinner party;
That we were uninvited, I am extremely sorry.
The mink was so delighted I'm afraid she over-ate.
It'll be many months until we have an omelet steaming on our plate.

10. *In the morning we found what mischief had been done,*
Out came the smoke bombs, steel traps and guns.
After a tramp through the woods we located the den
Will that midnight marauder ever maraud again?

11. *Although we dug and destroyed her hole in the ground,*
Not a single trace of the hunted criminal was found.
Except perhaps if you call this a trace:
A poor mangled duck her doorstep did grace.

12. *We all stood around with a shotgun or two,*
Each pair of eyes trained on the hole like glue.
The wind whipped us mercilessly but to no avail,
Despite even frostbite, justice must prevail.
Deep in a snow bank the minks' hole was concealed
So dad dug with the skid loader until the bottom was revealed.

13. *Watching every move our fingers were ready*
But shaking with cold I was far from steady.
I guess it was just as well she was not at home,
since my knees were so shaky and my hands felt like stone.

14. *She must have been watching us in hiding I think,*
For who can be sneakier than a seasoned mink?
Perhaps she has moved on and found a cozier den.
I'm willing to bet it's not far from some hens.

15. *To tell you the truth I'm inclined to believe,*
That it must have been fright that did away with the thief.
Such a large display of artillery would make me want to scram,
And she didn't stick around to witness the "BAM".

16. *But before she took leave she spent a few nights*
Eluding dad's traps and stealing bait-bites.
Who knows better than she the ways of a trap?
And how when they freeze down, they can't possibly snap!

17. *Here's a good bit of news that made our long faces glad,*
We've ordered some little chicks to replace the hens that we had.
They're so fluffy and cute and there's only one thing to regret,
They can't lay a single egg-as of yet.
But our punishment is deserved, of locking doors it has made us think,
For what use is an empty hen-house and a plumb full mink?

18. *One more words my friends, before I say adieu:*
The mink is still at large; of this I must warn you!
Be sure to keep your chickens locked up very tight,
Or else move them into your bedroom, where they'll be safe at night.

CHAPTER 17
New Gal's on the Farm

There are some new gals on the Callens Farm, folks. The lovely plump ladies, with every hair color imaginable, all belong to a certain club or organization of some sort. It's called "Sowies" and even though these gals don't always get along, they sure stick together when the chips are down. It seems that when this bunch of 11 arrived, they were all expecting, so now the club house that they all share is full of little ones. Would you like to meet our new friends? If you'll just step this way into this cozy little bungalow/barn, I'll introduce these wonderful ladies to you.

See how they all have their own bed? It is of the finest bedding-sweet golden straw. Now for the introductions: This on my right, in bed#1 is Rufus. (I know, it's an outlandish name... but wait until you hear some of the other distinguished ladies' titles!) Rufus has lovely red hair and it appears that many of her nine adorable babies have inherited it. Personally, she is my favorite of this remarkable group, even if she does growl when you come too close to her territory. She seems to have a special knack for "mothering" and by the way her babies rush to dinner, I'm under the impression that her milk is very sweet.

Here in bed #2 we have Dixie. It seems that large families are the norm with this group of "Sowies", and Dixie is not out of place with her troop of 14. Aren't her plump little roly-poly babies adorable? It seems that Dixie likes to nap quite regularly, so we won't tarry near her bed any longer in case we disturb her. And this is our newest mother, Bonnie in bed #3. She likes to play favorites I'm told, and while she won't allow Maple, another fellow "Sowie" near her 8 precious darlings, Tinker her next door neighbor is always welcome. A bit choosy don't you think? Perhaps the friendship between Tinker and Bonnie has something to do with their similar hair coloring. It's a rather dappled sort of color.... but then that seems to be the fashion with some of these ladies.

Tinker has 10 babies of her own and claims bed #4. Dorcas resides near Tinker in bed #5 and is the proud mother of 11! My! What a handsome brood she has! She is a very careful mother and takes extra pains not to lie on her babies. Dorcas is also very calm and is quite content to eat most of the time. A neutral member of the club, she takes no sides and her placid nature is accepted readily since some of the other ladies have rather unpredictable tempers.

On the other side of the room we have some very interesting characters indeed! Shhh.... this bed we are approaching belongs to the meanest of them all- the tough Bub. Don't get too close now; she has been known to charge at anyone who trespasses on her property. I wouldn't pet one of her brood if I were you. If any one of them squeals she will be upon you in no time! And remember what I said about those "Sowies" sticking together? If any baby squeals, they all rush out of their beds in search of the villain. And of course it will be you and I, for we are definitely outsiders aren't we? (Maybe you had better remove that ridiculous hat, it makes you look villainous!) Let's get away from Bub and her 11 kiddies while we can; right now we're sitting ducks! It's funny that two such ornery ladies could be neighbors. Then again, think how many such women could live on the same street, or in the same town..... But that's a different story.

Big Mamma in bed #7 really fits her name quite well. Take a look at those muscular shoulders and legs! I don't think we should mess with her my friend; she's already giving us the evil eye. Quick though, take a peak at her little ones, there are 10 of them! Uh oh! Why is that one squealing?! Look out! (Bang! Umph! "Run *now*!" "Over the fence!" " Whew!") Why in the world did you *stop* to ask me if the chips where down?! Look at them all glowering at us! Don't you know a mad "Sowie" when you see one? There's really nothing quite like it. All I can say, is I'm glad that they are on the other side of this railing! We made it just in time too. Really, this fine carpeting isn't meant for sneakers.....next time you visit our new residents why don't you wear boots? (Get the kind with grips on them-you never know when we'll have to make a fast getaway!) Let's venture out again; they seem to have calmed down. How are your heart palpitations? Better? Well what are we waiting for?!

Ah, here is Maple who is delicate in health at the moment. Some of her original 14 babies were sent out to be fostered by stronger "Sowie" members who had more milk, but she still has 7 cuddling with her. I'm sure they are a comfort to her as the other ladies treat her quite dreadfully. They seem to delight in picking on the weaker "Sowies". Lately Maple has had the treat of breakfast in bed due to her fragile condition. Maybe the other ladies are jealous?

Yes, this one is a pretty one isn't she? (I'm afraid beauty is only skin deep in this case) ZeBlue is not at all a good mother. Everyone had high hopes for this stylish "Sowie" but she has disappointed the whole group with her incompetence and selfishness. ZeBlue gave birth to 14 lovely babies, but due to a lack of consideration on her part, she made her bed on top of 7 of them. Their funeral was a sad event indeed. Needless to say, there is no love lost between our family and this unfeeling "Sowie". I can see breakfast sausage and pork chops looming in her future.

Now *here* is an admirable member of the "Sowie" club! Tough De De is definitely a tough mamma, but then tough love is the way to go isn't it? I've never seen a more gentle mother unless it's Rufus or Tough De De's neighbor Reddy. All three of them have a special quality about them. Tough De De is a bit smaller than the other ladies, but seriously, I wouldn't want to rub her the wrong way. (I don't think she likes being rubbed on the snout, why don't you try her back.)

And then there's this quiet, faithful, lady in our last bed #11. It's Reddy and look how she is snuggling with her 13 darlings. My! What a large brood! She is also a flaming red-head like Rufus across the hall. Is there something to these red haired ladies? So docile, (unless you make their babies squeal) so quiet, (until some member of the club needs defending) so cheerful, (unless dinner is late) and such good mothers! Would you like to hold one of these babies? Yes, I think I can get one from Reddy without getting hurt. Will she think I'm an invading "Sowie"?!! Hey, is that a hint? Look, if you pick the baby up by the leg carefully, they won't squeal. Aww....it's so soft! See, he's trying to root at your coat. Isn't it neat the way every baby has different colored hair? This one has polka dots! (Maybe that's the latest fad among the "Sowies" babies)

Say, I've heard that these little youngsters have already started a club of their own. Well, really they prefer to call it a *gang-* the Pigletto Bandits. These innocent looking piggies (short for Pigletto) have been known to sneak into the bed of an unsuspecting "Sowie" and steal the milk from the runts, *right* under their very snouts! Speaking of runts, you have to take a peak at this adorable little guy. Wilbur is Tough De De's little piggie. See his tiny button nose? He can fit right in your hand. Not many people can look good in polka-dots, but Wilbur is an exception to the rule.

Well I don't know about you, but it's 7 below, and my feet are nearing the glacial stage. Shall we head into the house and sit near the woodstove? What?! You want to start the tour all over again? *Do* be realistic! Bub might act up at any minute! That settles it? Ok, let's go. Goodbye my dear "Sowies"!

CHAPTER 18
Christmas in the Country

The soft glow of colored Christmas lights glimmer on the freshly fallen snow and the scent of wood smoke are in the air. Tall pines make a lovely backdrop for the gently falling snowflakes and the Christ Child smiles from his place amidst the animals of our outdoor Nativity scene. One of the children shouts happily and laughter rings through the air as someone is tossed from their sled into the soft snow. Christmastime has come once again to our farm, and it's just as lovely as it has always been.

There's something so special about spending this time of year in the country. The woodstove in the basement creates glowing warmth and is the coziest place in the house to sit and meditate over a cup of coffee or tea. Such a pleasant place to visit, arguments and misunderstandings are soon forgotten when seated around the stove. Before going out for chores in the cold morning, we gather around the stove to toast our fingers and toes before taking the plunge into the frosty air. Back in again we come with rosy cheeks and a hearty appetite. Mom usually has a steaming pot of warm coffee milk waiting and it's just the right thing to start the day.

Skating is another enjoyable holiday pastime. "The Pond" is only 1/2 mile from our home and is frequently the setting for fun and laughter. Bright faces match the colorful scarves and mittens as we skim round and round on the ice breathing in the fresh air. I often think of what a lovely postcard the skating children would make.

Star, our pony also takes part in the Christmas season. Good old fashioned sleigh rides are still as enjoyable as ever, and I suspect Star takes part in the amusement wholeheartedly. With a toss of her head she skims over the snow like a winged creature, her little hooves keeping time to our happy voices. Perhaps even more satisfactory to the pony, is the special treatment she gets after the sleigh ride. After all, it is the Christmas season is it not? A bit of extra corn won't hurt her, and she looks quite like a new pony after her careful grooming.

I wouldn't be surprised if the farm animals looked forward to Christmas just as much as we do. They enjoy the decorations and lights with the delight of little children. The kittens take in the Christmas lights shining from the tree with wide eyes. On many a night they sit at the window and gaze through at the family within. Playfully they scratch at the window, meowing to be let in. Susie our faithful dog holds above all else however, the Nativity scene in the front yard. What a precious sight to see her night after night curled up beside the Holy Family, trying to keep warm near the glowing lights. Was there a dog in that scene so long ago on the first Christmas night? Perhaps a sheep dog accompanied the shepherds on their pilgrimage to the manger. Susie seems to think she belongs there, and snuggles in her nest of straw.

Cookie baking time comes, and we have so much fun creating a variety of things. The little children like cut-out cookies the best, as they get to help with those. The heavenly aromas of chocolate, lemon, coconut and coffee mingle in the warm kitchen as we sing carols to the radio. Biscotti, Sugar cookies, Peanut Butter Blossoms, Lady Fingers and Tea Rocks are all packed away and frozen to be enjoyed throughout the weeks before Christmas. My mom bakes her traditional Italian Pizzelles similar to Belgian cookies with my grandmother's original iron. While the Christmas goose is saved for Christmas Day dinner with all of the relatives, we have our own little meal

here on Christmas Eve. This is such a special tradition to me and as Italian dainties are placed before us in the glow of candles we thank God for His many blessings.

I wonder of other Christmases spent in this old house and the surrounding homes long ago. Maybe there were years not so plentiful for the families that lived here before us. Probably their heads bowed in thanksgiving just the same for their meager fare. Maybe there were happier times when the rooms echoed with laughter as the carpets were rolled back for an old fashioned dance. Did the barns house teams decked with jangling harnesses and twinkling bells? Perhaps cheerful fiddle music drifted on the night air to the animals snug in their stalls. Was hot apple cider sipped from tin mugs after a sleigh ride over the fields? Maybe mistletoe hung in the doorway and fresh garlands wreathed the windows. And of course when all the happy caroling voices died away, there must have been a light in the window, welcoming the most important Guest of all.

Before the country was settled, perhaps Christmas came to a rude cabin dwelling where a happy family popped corn over a cheery blaze and ignored the chill winds seeping through cracks in the walls. There too, a light must have fallen across the snow through the window, welcoming the Baby Jesus.

Young families begin traditions that will be passed on from generation to generation; grandparents remember wonderful times spent with their children during the holidays and in turn share cherished memories with their grandchildren. What a delightful season this is! May you enjoy it to the fullest, keeping the simple pleasures close to your heart. Merry Christmas!

CHAPTER 19
A Christmas Goose

The center of attention, he will lie on a platter in the middle of the table with little white booties on the ends of his drumsticks. Quite lovely with that crispy golden-brown crust he is going to look in the light of the candles, but I know he'll taste even better. And when the Christmas dinner is over, all that will remain of that plump goose is his bones. Far away will be the days when he waddled the farm with his comrades, and nibbled at corn kernels. And most probably goose butchering day will be far from my mind by then; but as of now, it's still a fresh memory.

Mom picked the coldest day of the month to select and butcher a Christmas goose. The raw wind whipped at our clothes and stung our cheeks as we got the water boiling on a portable gas heater and set up the cutting tables. While the blades were being sharpened, mom looked over the flock. In fact, everyone put in their two cents. "Ahh! There is a plump one!" "Wait........ This one seems a bit more tender looking." "What about this young one here. He would be the perfect Christmas goose!" Well let me tell you folks, in the end, we selected not one, but *10* Christmas geese. Of course we couldn't eat them *all* for the Holiday, but they would be used throughout the winter. I must admit that the thought of cleaning 10 geese on such a cold day was not exactly pleasant, but then, would Christmas be pleasant without that golden brown goose?

We went to work with a will, some plucking feathers, others dunking the birds. If you've ever tried to pluck a goose, you'll know what I mean when I say that those feathers were plain *stubborn.* Easy, were the fine downy feathers that make goose-down pillows, but the others were a different story. We had quite a fun time tossing feathers at each other, and began to look ridiculously like fluffy geese ourselves. (Goose-down seems to stick rather easily to clothing.) Somehow the subject turned to tar-and-feathering- which of course, dad explained above all the teasing, was not a nice thing to do. I looked meaningfully at my sister and asked just how long the tar was supposed to keep the feathers on an individual.

As the wind grew stronger, our fingers and feet grew increasingly numb. I was thankful for the shelter of the pole barn; at least that protected us from most of the wind. After the plucking was far enough along, I commenced to cleaning the birds. Since I hadn't butchered since summer, it took a few birds for me to get back into practice, but soon drumsticks and gizzards were flying from goose to bowl. I did get quite a shock though and was not the only one, as my scream brought everyone running to see if I had been cut. That was not the case at all however. It seemed that I squeezed or sliced a little too close to some area and the dead goose's reaction was to "go" right on my coat front. Later on when it happened a second time, I just grimaced and shrugged my shoulders instead of screaming. There's no controlling a dead goose!

When I had a bowl full of clean meat, I headed for the house and up the basement stairs to bring it to mom for packaging. I guess it was my unlucky day with a twice stained coat and now *this*. (I can't really call it a catastrophe, because the geese came out ok.) After being outdoors, the basement appeared very dim and I didn't notice someone's boots lying right on the stairs. You guessed it- I tripped on them and fell down! My knee seemed to be the only bruised member and the tears I shed were from the uncontrollable laughter that followed the accident. And would you believe it? I didn't spill one goose out of that bowl!

At long last all the geese were plucked and clean, but the job was far from done. There was another party that rather seemed to need plucking and cleaning, and that was the bedraggled butchering crew. (Observing the way that feathers stuck onto people without aid, I was positive that I didn't need to use tar at all.) Yes, it was a tired and hungry crew that sat around the dining room table that Saturday night; hungry for *anything* but goose. Mom decided to sample a bit of goose meat for

Sunday dinner however, so that evening, one was selected for the crock and set to cooking. Sunday morning came, and the goose was still not finished. Whatever was the matter? After all night it should have been tender and juicy. Dinner time soon arrived but instead of the ideal plump drumsticks swimming in gravy, I'm afraid our goose looked rather like bits of leather floating in salty water. Everyone turned to mom for an explanation and a slow smile of realization broke over her face. It seems that out of all 10 geese, she had accidentally chosen the very oldest, toughest one of all. In all truth, there *was* a bright side to that Sunday meal as we tried to gnaw the leather-like meat; at least there was no chance of having *this* old geezer for Christmas dinner!

And when I see that Christmas goose in all his splendor amidst dear family faces gathered 'round, I know I won't regret the work (and the fun) it took to set him upon the platter.

CHAPTER 20
'Tis The Season

It's that beautiful time of year again, the time of anticipation and preparation for the Christmas season. Although I'll admit that winter is my least favorite season of the year, Christmas is definitely my favorite holiday. And in our family it's a time of togetherness, excitement, warmth and well, also a bit of chaos. Whether it's cookie baking or "decking the halls", everybody wants to get involved.

This year the girls and I were extremely eager to start up the cookie baking. A few weeks ago we shopped for cookie cutters, sprinkles, nuts, chocolate chips, candies and whatever else that needed to be re-stocked before we started up. Of course that was a lot of fun! Soon the cupboards bulged with a little of this and a little of that, and we were pretty well satisfied that cookie baking could now commence. We were ready. Besides, mom had that "enough is enough" look on her face. We donned aprons and with blissful importance thumbed through the cookbook gazing upon all the gorgeous pictures of Peanut Blossoms, Gingerbread Men, Twisted Wreath's and Chocolate Stuffed Cookie Stockings. Our eyes widened and we could almost smell the delectable aroma of the Pecan Tassies and Cream Cheese Tarts shown at the back of the book.

I suppose it took us a good half hour to choose which cookie to try first but in the end it was Gingerbread Men that took first place (probably because of the element of decorating) and we mixed, sifted and poured until we had a nice dough. Actually it was a bit dry to begin with, but I took care of that with an extra egg. The younger girls were impressed with my resourcefulness and my explanation that the dough should become a trifle sticky at this point seemed to satisfy them. It wasn't until we eagerly dug out the cookie cutters and rolling pins that I found out the dough needed chilling. What a tough break! And three whole hours! Well, that wasn't going to stop us!

No one wanted to hang up their aprons so we dug in again-this time into the peanut butter. Yes, while our Gingerbread dough chilled in the refrigerator (we wanted to put it in the freezer but mom said that wouldn't do) we mixed up a batch of Peanut Blossoms. Our first batch looked beautiful (almost as nice as the batch pictured in the Better Homes and Gardens cookbook) although we did make the mistake of replacing hard shortening with vegetable oil. We decided that the batch was too small and mixed up yet another. As I opened up a bag of chocolate kisses to press into the middle of the cookies, my three littlest siblings stood with noses pressed onto the counter edge making puppy eyes. I tried my best to ignore the fact that their open mouths greatly resembled those of hungry little birds in the springtime.

By the time the Peanut Blossoms were finished and the chocolate kisses safely stowed out of sight, the Gingerbread dough was sufficiently chilled. I'll never know why we decided to do Sugar Cookie cut-outs AND Gingerbread cut-outs all in one day, but I guess we thought that Gingerbread Men alone wouldn't be enough to decorate. For that was really what we had been anticipating all this time. The delightful job of mixing food coloring into frosting, sprinkling the little snowflakes, colored sugars and shapes all over the cookies, yes that was what we were waiting for. And when you're going to decorate why not decorate in large quantities?

Us two oldest girls decided that we had better do most of the decorating since the younger kids made rather messy "designs". But after an hour or two and the mounds of cookies still looked to be about the same height, we gave in and let the twins help out. And finally when the pleading puppy eyes got too big to resist, three more little kids were sitting proudly around the table slathering on frosting and dumping on sprinkles. Although we hardly had any elbow room, it was still fun! We passed around bowls of frosting at alarming rates and every time our favorite Christmas carol came on the radio we'd crank it up and sing at the top of our voices.

The warm smells of baking cookies and the smiling faces (however streaked with frosting they were) of family were lovely and the next afternoon we were at it again. You may think that the gentlemen of the family did not have a part in the festivities but they did. Self appointed "taste-testers" they were, and kept appearing to sample each new batch of cookies and every different color of frosting! By the time all the cookies were decorated (or at least covered with some sort of multi-colored coating) our backs and necks were stiff from bending over the table and there were many visions of Gingerbread Men "dancing in our heads" that night as we tumbled gratefully into bed.

Well, we've still been baking (mom even experimented on the little Pecan Tassies) but our latest holiday adventure has been putting up the tree and lights. I mentioned one Sunday afternoon that it might be a good day to do it, and after that there was no peace. Snuggled in the rocker reading a book: "Jessi, can we put up the tree now?" Strolling around the yard to get some oxygen: "Jessi, mom said to ask you if you can help us set up the tree now." Closing my eyes for a cat-nap: "Jessi, is it time yet?" "Are we going to do it today?" I really was almost as excited about it as the younger kids and finally after chores we hauled the old artificial tree down the attic steps.

Although maybe it wasn't quite as exciting as hauling a real live tree across an open field of snow after selecting it and cutting it down, we did feel a spirit of camaraderie as we searched together for the old tree among boxes, bags and books in the attic. And it was fun watching our brother carry it down the steep stairs. It took quite a lot of muscle to lift the tree over the guard rail along the stairs, and as Clayton stumbled over the bag of clothes sitting on the bottom step, we erupted in giggles and he stared at us indignantly through the branches of greenery.

I always liked trimming the tree in the evening; there is something so cozy about it. Maybe it's because the lights glimmer better, and that's probably why I made the kids wait until evening. We had a great time, the little kids spreading ornaments crazily here and there, the older kids organizing them when they weren't looking. Strings of blinking lights were strewn over the floor and dining room chairs all over the living room as we climbed up to hang a long row of stockings. Midway, we got a unanimous craving for fudge (interesting how we get these entire family cravings. It's like that with pop-corn too.) and mom and I whipped up a batch and stuck it in the refrigerator to cool down. I put up the garland above the living room entrance three times because Bella kept pulling it down and I still think it looks rather uneven. Oh well, she was happy standing up on that chair helping me.

Somewhere in the process of setting up the Nativity, Caleb decapitated a Wise-Man (last year it was a shepherd and the year before, a lamb...) and once again dad has taken out the Elmer's glue and raised another figurine to life. Hopefully we'll be able to keep the most important figures intact. Maybe it's a good thing baby Jesus doesn't make an appearance until Christmas.

This year we even strung lights out side. We don't get much traffic, but it's a thrill for us to come home from an evening away and see the colored bulbs shining that welcoming, festive glow. It's been our family tradition for years to watch the classic movie "It's A Wonderful Life" before Christmas. It teaches such a beautiful lesson on the importance of every single human being. When the film is over I know I'm not the only one in the room with wet eyes. Mom and dad usually get us to watch the old black and white "Scrooge" too before Christmas. Another movie with a good lesson. It doesn't frighten me as much as when I was little but I still come away determined to be less selfish, for who wants to become a Scrooge anyway?

Aaah....Christmas 'tis the season isn't it? A season of fun, fudge and celebration, but most of all a time of family togetherness and preparation. Not only preparation of festive décor and Christmas goodies, but the preparation of our hearts. May not only our homes shine in readiness of the coming holiday, but may our hearts also reflect warmth, beauty and welcome for the baby Jesus. And may He bless you this Christmas season in a very special way. Merry Christmas!

CHAPTER 21
He Was Laid in Our Manger

'...She wrapped him in swaddling clothes and laid him in a manger, because there was no room for them in the inn...' So where did they go? To the stable, and that is the greatest event in animal history.

Ahh... the great Christmas story. How I so love to hear it! It never gets old, especially since, around Christmas time out here in the barn, one will hear many different accounts of the ancient story. But I am neglecting my manners! Allow me to introduce myself. I am Fuzzwald the sheep. Ladies and gentleman, I am about to present you with a Christmas story from the perspective of an animal and, (as that admirable specimen of humanity, Mr. Paul Harvey puts it,) "the ressst of the story".

Now then, would you care to hear a few of those different accounts of the Christmas story that I spoke of a minute ago? The cow Bernadette tells us it went this way, "His mooother wrapped him in swaddling clooothes and laid him in the manger of the jersey cooow which was warmed by her breath and strewn with wisps of her soooft hay." All of the geese agree that it was this way, "She wrapwrapwrapped him in swas-waswaddling clothes and laid him in a manger full of goose down." Ahh yes, and Jake and Brandy the dogs insist that it goes, "She wrapped him in (woof!) swaddling clothes and laid him (woof!) in a manger while the dog kept watch at the stable door (woof!)" (They never can agree on what breed the dog was; a Golden Lab or a Springer Spaniel!) Of course the hens say that it was a chicken who clucked Him to sleep and those high headed horses claim that their breed was the first to kneel and adore…

What do I say? I don't have to say anything, you see. It's all in the original story; the best part of the tale if you don't mind my saying. Listen, my friends: 'Now there were shepherds in that region living in the fields and keeping the night watch over their flock (it was a flock of sheep you see). The angel of the Lord appeared to them and the glory of the Lord shone around them, and they were struck with great fear. The angel said to them, "Do not be afraid; for behold, I proclaim to you good news of great joy that will be for all the people.' Ah HA! It was a flock of sheep (my ancestors no doubt) that along with the shepherds, were the very first to hear the great tidings from the angel of the Lord! But that's not all! '…they went in haste (most likely taking along a young lamb or two that was certain to wander in their absence) and found Mary and Joseph, and the infant lying in the manger.'

Now, from that very night, sheep all around the world have passed on this little addition to the story from generation to generation, although grandbaaa always said that it was but an error on the part of the disciples that it was omitted from the gospels! 'It came to pass that a cold night wind blew through the low door of the stable and the shepherds, seeing that the babe had only swaddling clothes, bade the lambs to cuddle with the child and keep him warm with their thick wool.' My, aren't we sheep a privileged breed!

But we animals aren't the only ones preparing for the beautiful Christmas season! We take quite a bit of interest in the preparations and activities going on over at the big house of the farmer and his family. We hear music! Christmas concerts 24/7! I heard from Jake that they even have a church organ in the dining room! Imagine that! No wonder those stucco walls vibrate! Practice, practice, practice. We love our musical farm family… although we seldom have any peace and quiet!

Jessica rushes out of the house almost every Tuesday night at precisely 7:00 and sits impatiently in the car as her siblings trail slowly out one after another. Must be Christmas choir practice night! Once in a while the little kids come out and sled down the snow mounds their daddy made in the middle of the yard. I'm glad that their enthusiasm has finally been directed to something other than mutton busting. Folks, when little kids get it in their head that they're gonna be a pro-sheep rider, the last thing you want to be is a sheep! But where was I…Oh! I was about to tell about the preparations for Christmas dinner.

It makes my wool curl just to think about it, but I've begun, and there's nothing to do but go ahead and tell. The farmers family, they (shhh..come closer) selected and uhh.. exterminated (may he rest in peace) a goose! (I guess it must be difficult to rest in peace without your feathers. Poor fella…) Just one more reason to be glad you're a sheep! That is, until Easter time comes around. Some people have horrible traditions! A few weeks before Christmas, the outdoor nativity scene and colored lights go up. From my pen here in the barn I can just about see every piece glowing in the darkness and it makes my fluffy self warm with gladness to see those plastic sheep set in their proper places close beside the sleeping infant. Somebody around here knows what they're doing!

The scent of Christmas goodies floats out through the stove vent and my, what a treat! Candies and fudge, even cookies that resemble men, so the cat says! She saw them from her perch near the kitchen window! (How anyone could eat a model of their own kind is beside me…) All that stuff smells mighty good and I'm usually content with my feed and hay but I'll admit that once in a while around Christmas time I find myself wishing I were human. But then I'm reminded of that grand privilege only an animal may have on Christmas Eve, and I wouldn't trade places with any two legged creature on earth!

The sun sets on Christmas Eve and the family hurries through chores. One thing about that family, they sure are dedicated to their animals! Why, no matter where they are going, or what the occasion may be, they always make sure that we are well fed and bedded. One of those twins even slipped us some extra hay tonight for a Christmas treat. Twins sure are special-I ought to know! The house is ablaze with lights and someone is doing some last minute organ practice. 6:00 pm arrives and they scurry out of the house and pack themselves into that 12 passenger van. By golly, they even have room for one more! Headlights pierce the darkness about an hour later and the family heads in for (gulp-may he rest in peace) the goose.

The hours tick by and all of us animals wait expectantly for the hour of midnight. The cat has her eye on the kitchen clock and she's to relay the message to Jake who will bark twelve times to announce the greatest moment of the year for animals everywhere. A reverent hush falls over the barn at the bark of midnight and a glow descends upon us all. There is the most beautiful sight you have ever seen! Mary, Joseph and the lovely baby boy nestled in the straw while angels hover 'round singing sweetly. We kneel and adore the infant who became the Messiah, the Sacrificial Lamb, healer, teacher, Prince of Peace, the Good Shepherd.

What a wonderful thing it is to be an animal on Christmas Eve! Mary once told us that it is in thanksgiving for the generosity of those kind animals of so long ago, that on every Christmas Eve the Holy Family appears to all of the animals around the world. O Come let us Adore Him!

ABOUT THE AUTHOR

JESSICA ANET CALLENS has been a writer ever since she put on her first pair of overalls and began to help with the family chores. At age seven she began writing short stories and poems and 2 years later at the age of nine, joined a writing club and began to write her own books. Even at an early age Jessica was inspired by the charm, humor and wisdom found in ordinary every day life and was able to write about it. In 2001 Jessica began writing stories for her hometown newspaper, many of which are included in this book.

Aside from writing, Jessica is a musician and has spent many years competing in various state competitions on both the organ and piano. She graduated from high-school in the spring of 2005 and currently plays organ and directs the choir in her home parish of   St. Leo's in St. Leo, MN. Jessica also teaches piano lessons and performs around SW Minnesota with *THE CALLENS FAMILY ENTERTAINERS* playing the fiddle, accordion, guitar and keyboard. Reading, riding horse, baking and listening to Country music are other things she enjoys with her eight brothers and sisters.

Jessica understands the importance of sharing real life experiences with people everywhere and continues to find plenty of writing material while doing chores on the 17 acre family farm. Jessica plans to continue writing a series on the rural lifestyle that she loves so well.

JOIN US TODAY
DOWN ON THE FARM

FREE BONUS!

Visit *http://www.Morgan-James.com/farm* to view

the FREE movie slideshow and tour the entire

CALLENS FARM through MORE beautiful photographs!

HTTP://WWW.MORGAN-JAMES.COM/FARM